QUICK FROM SCRATCH
Vegetable Main Dishes

Gado Gado, page 147

QUICK FROM SCRATCH
Vegetable Main Dishes

American Express Publishing Corporation
New York

Editor in Chief: Judith Hill

Art Director: Nina Scerbo   **Managing Editor:** Terri Mauro
Designer: Leslie Andersen   **Associate Editor:** Laura Byrne Russell
Photographer: Melanie Acevedo   **Copy Editor:** Barbara A. Mateer
Food Stylist: Rori Spinelli   **Editorial Assistant:** Evette Manners
Prop Stylist: Robyn Glaser   **Contributing Editor:** Catherine Young
Wine Editor: Steve Miller

Production Manager: Yvette Williams-Braxton

———

Vice President, Consumer Marketing: Mark V. Stanich
Vice President, Books and Information Services: John Stoops
Marketing Director: Tom Reynolds
Operations Manager: Doreen Camardi
Business Manager: Joanne Ragazzo

———

Recipes Pictured on Cover: (Front) Asparagus and Bok-Choy Frittata, page 91
(Back) Vegetable Chili with Garlic Rice, page 71;
Inset top: Spaghetti with Escarole and Bacon, page 53;
Inset bottom: Eggplant and Goat-Cheese "Sandwiches" with Tomato Tarragon Sauce, page 105
Page 6: *Portraits:* Chris Dinerman

Special thanks to Charles Balducci, of Balducci's in New York City,
for help in developing the Vegetable Seasons chart on pages 180-181.

AMERICAN EXPRESS PUBLISHING CORPORATION
©1998 American Express Publishing Corporation

LIBRARY OF CONGRESS CATALOGING-IN-PUBLICATION DATA
Quick from scratch. Vegetable main dishes.
p.   cm.
Includes index.
ISBN 0-916103-49-8
1. Cookery (Vegetables) 2. Entrées (Cookery) 3. Quick and easy cookery. I. Food & wine (New York, N.Y.)

TX801.Q58 1998

641.6'5—dc21   98-8309
                                                            CIP

Published by American Express Publishing Corporation
1120 Avenue of the Americas, New York, New York 10036

Manufactured in the United States of America

CONTENTS

RECIPES PICTURED ABOVE: (*left to right*) pages 73, 93, 105

Choosing our favorite shots during a photography session for this book.

 *Judith Hill* is the editor in chief of FOOD & WINE Books, a division of American Express Publishing. Previously she was editor in chief of COOK'S Magazine, director of publications for La Varenne École de Cuisine in Paris, from which she earned a Grand Diplôme, and an English instructor for the University of Maryland International Division in Germany. Her book credits include editing cookbooks for Fredy Girardet, Jane Grigson, Michel Guérard, and Anne Willan.

 *Laura Byrne Russell* earned a bachelor's degree in finance and worked in stock and bond sales for a few years before deciding that food is more fun. She went back to school, this time to The Culinary School at Kendall College in Illinois. After gaining experience in professional kitchens in Chicago and New York City, she came to FOOD & WINE Books, where she works as both an editor and a recipe developer.

My Name Is Judith, and I'm an Omnivore

Right up front, I want to say that I'm omnivorous. I enjoy virtually everything there is on earth to eat (which is why I'm in the food business, also why my hips are bigger than I'd like). And I especially relish meat. So does Laura Russell, who so ably developed most of the recipes in this book.

Yet we both find that we're cooking fewer meals than we used to that feature meat as the centerpiece. We go home after work and make a quick pasta dish, a stir-fry, a risotto, maybe a big salad, much more often than we cook a steak, a chop, a roast, even a piece of chicken or fish. The balance has shifted: One-dish meals with a lot of *vegetables and a little meat* (or no meat at all) have become more typical, for us anyway, than *MEAT* with vegetables on the side.

We think this is true of many of our readers as well, and hence this book. It's crammed with ideas for fast, vegetable-based dishes that are dinners in themselves.

But this is not a vegetarian cookbook. We couldn't live without chicken stock, for one thing, and we often flavor our vegetables with a bit of bacon or tuna or sausage or whatever meaty tidbits we have on hand. That said, the recipes here that aren't vegetarian can easily become so by simply omitting any morsel of meat we've included or replacing chicken stock with vegetable stock (page 183), plain water, or wine.

Whether we're doing without meat altogether or just changing our meal-planning emphasis from animals to plants, we all still want—thank heavens—to enjoy delicious food. We at FOOD & WINE Books hope that this volume in our *Quick from Scratch* series will help you to do just that.

Judith Hill
Editor in Chief
FOOD & WINE Books

8

Before You Begin

You'll find test-kitchen tips and ideas for ingredient substitutions presented with the individual recipes throughout *Quick from Scratch: Vegetable Main Dishes*. In this opening section, we've gathered information and tips that apply to all, or at least a substantial number, of the recipes. These are the facts and opinions that we'd like you to know before you use the recipes and to keep in mind while you use them. The culinary information here will help make your cooking quicker, simpler, and tastier.

Faster, Better, Easier
TEST-KITCHEN TIPS

Selecting vegetables

Whether in your supermarket's produce aisle or at your local farmers' market, fresh vegetables should look firm, plump, and as if they're bursting with life. Avoid those that are dried out, bruised, discolored, or overly soft.

Washing, drying, and storing greens

■ Greens such as spinach, escarole, and lettuce can harbor tremendous amounts of dirt and sand. Often a simple rinsing isn't enough. To **clean** greens properly, fill the sink or a large bowl with water. Immerse the greens in the water, swish them around, and let the sediment sink to the bottom. Lift the greens from the water leaving the dirt behind, dump or drain the water, rinse the sink or bowl, and repeat until the greens are perfectly clean. This process may seem troublesome, but it's well worth the effort to avoid grittiness.

■ **Dry** the greens by giving them a whirl in a salad spinner, or drain them in a colander and then on paper towels. Greens intended for salads need to be especially dry, or the dressing won't cling. Of course, if you're about to steam or boil the greens, you don't need to dry them at all.

■ To **store** washed greens for a few hours, put them in a bowl, cover with a moist paper towel, and refrigerate. Unwashed greens do best when wrapped in paper towels, stuck in a plastic bag, and refrigerated.

RECIPES PICTURED OPPOSITE: *(top)* pages 161, 145, 133; *(center)* pages 33, 87, 19; *(bottom)* pages 111, 145, 85

9

Storing vegetables

- A cold, moist place—the refrigerator—is the best place for **most vegetables**. They'll stay hydrated enough to remain fresh for at least several days. Too much moisture leads to rot, though, so don't encase the vegetables in plastic wrap; perforated plastic bags are ideal. Mushrooms are particularly sensitive to moisture. Store them in a paper bag or a paper-towel-lined plastic bag.
- A cool, dry place, such as a pantry, is ideal for **potatoes, onions, garlic, winter squash,** and **sweet potatoes**. If you don't have such a place, choose the refrigerator over a room-temperature spot.
- Room temperature is perfect for juicy summer-ripe **tomatoes**; refrigeration makes them mealy. The only time you should ever refrigerate tomatoes is to prevent overripe ones from spoiling.

Ripening and keeping avocados

- Ripe avocados are unctuous, creamy, and flavorful; unripe avocados are none of the above. Not surprisingly, then, you'll want your avocados to be absolutely ripe. If you purchase one that's not, put it in a paper bag and keep it on the counter. As it ripens, the color will darken and the flesh will soften. When the avocado yields to gentle pressure, it's ready to use.
- Once cut, avocados brown quickly. Wait until the last minute to slice them, or toss the slices with something acidic, such as lemon or lime juice or vinegar. An avocado half that's still in its skin will keep quite well for a day or two. Rub the cut part with the acid of your choice, flatten plastic wrap directly on the surface, and refrigerate.

Cleaning mushrooms

Because fresh mushrooms are like sponges, it's best not to soak them or keep them under running water for too long. That doesn't mean you can't rinse them, though, just that you'll need to do it quickly.

Choosing a peeler

A waxy coating, stringy fibers, or simply personal preference—all are good reasons for peeling a vegetable. We find swivel-blade peelers especially effective (they flow along the various shapes of different vegetables and also keep a sharp edge well) but just about any paring knife or vegetable peeler will do the job.

Peeling potatoes

Whether you choose to peel potatoes or not is largely a matter of your own taste. If there is a greenish tint just under the skin, however, you'll want to peel it away completely. The green part is caused by prolonged exposure to light and can be mildly toxic if eaten in large quantities. Once peeled, the remainder of the potato is perfectly safe to eat.

Seeding tomatoes

The easiest way to remove tomato seeds is to halve the tomato horizontally, hold it cut-side down, squeeze gently, and scrape off the seeds with a quick swipe of your finger. Don't worry about getting rid of every last seed.

Preventing oxidation

Certain vegetables, such as artichokes, celery root, and Jerusalem artichokes, turn brown quickly after being peeled or cut; put the cut vegetables in a bowl of water with a squeeze of lemon juice added to it to help them hold their color. Cut potatoes will also turn brown but will do so less quickly. Keeping them in plain water is sufficient.

Precooking vegetables

Parboiling vegetables is a great way to get a head start on dinner. Boil the vegetables in a pot of boiling, salted water until they're nearly tender and then drain them. Put the partially cooked vegetables in a bowl of very cold water to stop the cooking. As soon as they've cooled down, drain them. Keep them at room temperature for a few hours, if you like, or store them in the refrigerator for longer periods. Just before serving, sauté the vegetables with a little butter or olive oil to reheat them and finish the cooking.

Cooking green vegetables

■ Please cook green vegetables until they're tender. You'll find they have so much more flavor than when still firm and fibrous, somewhere between raw and cooked, as they're so often served today. This is not to advocate overcooking to the point of olive-drab mush as used to be the norm. We've simply overcompensated and need to find a balance.

■ Cook vegetables in boiling, salted water. Not only does salt bring out the flavor of vegetables, it also helps them retain their color.

■ Boil green vegetables uncovered to preserve their color.

■ Don't add baking soda to the cooking water. It's an old trick to keep vegetables bright, but unfortunately, it also turns them to mush.

■ Steaming has long been praised as the most nutritious way to cook vegetables, but the vitamin loss in boiling has been overstated. The difference in vitamin content between boiled and steamed vegetables is infinitesimal.

Watch the cooking time

Though cooking times vary among vegetables, you don't have to make life difficult by cooking them in separate pots. When cooking different types together, you can add one to the pot sooner or cut it into smaller pieces so all will be done at the same time.

Frozen spinach

Since it's already been stemmed, cleaned, and cooked, using chopped or whole-leaf frozen spinach is a huge time-saver. Just be sure to remove all the moisture from the spinach before adding it to a dish. Drain defrosted spinach in a colander and then squeeze it dry, a handful at a time, until virtually no liquid remains.

ESSENTIAL INGREDIENT INFORMATION

Broth, Chicken

We tested the recipes in this book with canned low-sodium chicken broth. You can almost always substitute regular for low-sodium broth; just cut back on the salt in the recipe. And if you keep homemade stock in your freezer, by all means use it. We aren't suggesting that it won't work as well, only that we know the dishes taste delicious even when made with canned broth. If you'd prefer to substitute vegetable stock in any of these recipes, try our version on page 183.

Butter

Our recipes don't specify whether to use salted or unsalted butter. We generally use unsalted, but in these savory dishes, it really won't make a big difference which type you use.

Cheese, Grated

We frequently call for Parmesan cheese. Not only is it widely available, but it's hard to beat real fresh-grated Parmigiano-Reggiano. However, Parmesan has become something of a generic term including all Italian grating cheeses, and we use it in that sense. Feel free to substitute Romano or Asiago.

Citrus Juice

Many of our recipes call for lemon or lime juice. For a bright boost of flavor, use juice from fresh fruit. The bottled stuff just doesn't taste as good.

Coconut Milk

Coconut milk is the traditional liquid used in many Thai and Indian curries. Make sure you buy *unsweetened* canned coconut milk, not cream of coconut, which is used primarily for piña coladas. Heavy cream can be substituted in most recipes.

Ginger, Fresh

Fresh ginger, or gingerroot, is a knobby, tan-skinned rhizome found in the produce section of your supermarket. You need to peel its thin skin before using; this is most easily accomplished by scraping it with a spoon. After peeling, the ginger is ready to be grated, sliced, or chopped.

Mustard

By mustard, we mean a good one, such as Dijon. We never, ever mean yellow ballpark mustard.

Nuts

Our quick pantry wouldn't be complete without several kinds of nuts. Keep in mind that nuts have a high percentage of oil and can turn rancid quickly. We store ours in the freezer to keep them fresh.

Oil

Cooking oil in these recipes refers to readily available, reasonably priced nut, seed, or vegetable oil with a high smoking point, such as peanut, sunflower, canola, safflower, or corn oil. These can be heated to about 400° before they begin to smoke, break down, and develop an unpleasant flavor.

Parsley

Many of our recipes call for chopped fresh parsley. Unless we've specified otherwise, you can use either the flat-leaf or the curly variety.

Pepper

■ There's nothing like fresh-ground pepper. If you've been using preground, buy a pepper mill, fill it with peppercorns, and give it a grind. You'll never look back.

■ To measure your just-ground pepper more easily, become familiar with your own mill; each produces a different amount per turn. You'll probably find that ten to fifteen grinds produces one-quarter teaspoon of pepper, and then you can count on that forever after.

Tomatoes, Canned

In some recipes, we call for "crushed tomatoes in thick puree." Depending on the brand, this mix of crushed tomatoes and tomato puree may be labeled crushed tomatoes with puree, with added puree, in tomato puree, thick style, or in thick puree. You can use any of these.

Wine, Dry White

Leftover wine is ideal for cooking. It seems a shame to open a fresh bottle for just a few spoonfuls. Another solution is to keep dry vermouth on hand. You can use whatever quantity is needed; the rest will keep indefinitely.

Zest

Citrus zest—the colored part of the peel, without any white pith—adds tremendous flavor to many a dish. Remove the zest from the fruit using either a grater or a zester. A zester is a small, inexpensive, and extremely handy tool. It has little holes that remove just the zest in fine ribbons. A zester is quick, easy to clean, and never scrapes your knuckles.

CHAPTER ONE

Stir-Fries, Stews & Curries

VEGETABLE STIR-FRY WITH GINGER VINAIGRETTE

Fresh and green and bursting with flavor, this stir-fry is like a little taste of springtime that you can serve any time of year. Carrots, red bell pepper, or asparagus (if it really *is* springtime) will make the dish even prettier. Serve the medley with rice.

WINE RECOMMENDATION
Nothing enhances the flavors of Asian seasonings and fresh vegetables as well as riesling. Here, however, you can use a dry wine; a Rheingau trocken (dry) spätlese is a good choice.

SERVES 4

- 1 tablespoon minced fresh ginger
- 1 teaspoon lemon juice
- 3 tablespoons cooking oil
- 1 teaspoon Asian sesame oil
- ½ teaspoon salt
- ⅛ teaspoon fresh-ground black pepper
- 3 cloves garlic, minced
- 1 large head bok choy (about 1½ pounds), stalks cut into ½-inch pieces, leaves shredded
- ½ pound snow peas
- 10 radishes, quartered
- 4 teaspoons soy sauce
- ½ pound spinach, stems removed and leaves washed well
- ½ pound firm tofu, cut into ¾-inch dice

1. In a small glass or stainless-steel bowl, combine the ginger, lemon juice, 1 tablespoon of the cooking oil, the sesame oil, ¼ teaspoon of the salt, and the pepper. Set aside.

2. In a wok or a large nonstick frying pan, heat the remaining 2 tablespoons cooking oil over moderately high heat. Add the garlic and cook, stirring, until fragrant, about 10 seconds. Add the bok-choy stalks and cook, stirring, for 1 minute. Add the snow peas and cook, stirring, for 1 minute. Add the radishes and the soy sauce and cook, stirring, for 1 minute longer.

3. Add the bok-choy leaves, the spinach, and the remaining ¼ teaspoon salt to the pan. Cook, tossing gently, until the leaves just wilt, 1 to 2 minutes. Add all but 1 tablespoon of the vinaigrette and toss to coat. Remove the vegetables from the pan.

4. In the same pan, heat the remaining tablespoon of vinaigrette over moderately high heat. Add the tofu and cook, turning occasionally, until warmed through, about 2 minutes. Return the vegetables to the pan and stir gently to mix.

STIR-FRIED VEGETABLES WITH TOASTED CASHEWS

The crunch of the charred cashews and the meaty texture of the mushrooms are retained by cooking them separately and saving them for a topping instead of cooking them with the rest of the vegetables. Serve the stir-fry with either white or brown rice.

WINE RECOMMENDATION
Wines from Austria are more available than ever. Pick a grüner veltliner, a white wine with intriguing fruity and peppery flavors, for a tasty change of pace.

SERVES 4

3 tablespoons canned low-sodium chicken broth or homemade stock

1 teaspoon cornstarch

3 tablespoons cooking oil

²⁄₃ cup cashews

Dried red-pepper flakes

1 pound mushrooms, sliced thin

¹⁄₂ teaspoon salt

4 scallions, white bulbs sliced thin, green tops chopped and reserved separately

³⁄₄ teaspoon Asian sesame oil

3 cloves garlic, minced

1 pound broccoli, thick stems removed, tops cut into small florets (about 1 quart)

1¹⁄₂ pounds napa (Chinese) cabbage (about ¹⁄₂ head), shredded (about 1¹⁄₂ quarts)

1 tablespoon oyster sauce

2 tablespoons soy sauce

1. In a small bowl, combine 1 tablespoon of the broth with the cornstarch. In a wok or a large nonstick frying pan, heat ¹⁄₂ tablespoon of the cooking oil over moderately high heat. Add the cashews; cook, stirring, until starting to char, 1 to 2 minutes. Transfer the nuts to a medium bowl and add a pinch of red-pepper flakes.

2. In the same pan, heat 1 tablespoon of the cooking oil over moderately high heat. Add the mushrooms and ¹⁄₄ teaspoon of the salt and cook, stirring occasionally, until golden brown, about 5 minutes. Transfer to the bowl with the cashews. Stir the scallion greens and sesame oil into the mushroom mixture.

3. Heat the remaining 1¹⁄₂ tablespoons of cooking oil over moderately high heat. Add the scallion bulbs and garlic; cook, stirring, about 30 seconds. Add the broccoli and cook, stirring, for 1 minute. Add the cabbage; cook, stirring, until the cabbage wilts, about 2 minutes. Stir in the remaining 2 tablespoons broth and ¹⁄₄ teaspoon salt, ¹⁄₄ teaspoon red-pepper flakes, and the oyster and soy sauces. Stir the cornstarch mixture, add it to the pan, and bring to a boil. Cook, stirring, until the sauce coats the vegetables, about 1 minute. Serve topped with the mushroom mixture.

19

FIVE-VEGETABLE STIR-FRY WITH LENTILS

A dinner of Brussels sprouts, turnips, carrots, and lentils may sound more like a punishment than a treat, but believe us—the combination is delicious. In fact, the general effect is actually rather delicate.

WINE RECOMMENDATION

Here's a tip: When confronted with a wine list full of unknowns, look for an Alsace pinot blanc. It will go with almost anything, including this unusual stir-fry.

SERVES 4

½ cup lentils

3⅓ cups water

2½ teaspoons salt

3 tablespoons cooking oil

1 tablespoon minced fresh ginger

4 scallions including green tops, chopped

2 turnips, peeled, quartered, and sliced thin

3 carrots, sliced thin

3 tablespoons white-wine vinegar

1 tablespoon butter

¾ pound Brussels sprouts, trimmed and sliced

1 10-ounce package frozen cut green beans

1. In a medium saucepan, combine the lentils, 2 cups of the water, and ¾ teaspoon of the salt. Bring to a boil, reduce the heat, and simmer, partially covered, until the lentils are just tender but not falling apart, 25 to 30 minutes. Drain if necessary, cover, and set aside.

2. Meanwhile, in a large nonstick frying pan or a wok, heat 1 tablespoon of the oil over moderately high heat. Add half of the ginger and scallions and cook, stirring, for 30 seconds. Add the turnips and carrots and cook, stirring, for 2 minutes. Add 1 cup of the water, ¾ teaspoon of the salt, and the vinegar. Boil until the vegetables are tender and no liquid remains in the pan, about 10 minutes. Transfer the vegetables to a large bowl.

3. In the same pan, melt the butter with the remaining 2 tablespoons of oil over moderately high heat. Add the remaining ginger and scallions and cook, stirring, for 30 seconds. Add the Brussels sprouts and cook, stirring, for 2 minutes. Add the green beans and the remaining ⅓ cup of water and 1 teaspoon salt. Reduce the heat and simmer until the vegetables are just tender, about 5 minutes. Stir in the carrot mixture and the drained lentils and toss gently to combine.

KALE AND WHITE-BEAN STEW

Combining two Portuguese favorites—kale-and-sausage soup and a bean, sausage, and tomato stew—makes a simple, sensational one-pot meal. To keep the focus on the vegetables, we've used just a tiny amount of fresh sausage; you can add more, if you like, or substitute dried chorizo or pepperoni.

WINE RECOMMENDATION
Since this dish has a strong Portuguese influence, why not pair it with a rustic red from Portugal? Try one of the many delicious examples from the Douro or Ribatejo regions for a lusty combination of food and drink.

SERVES 4

2   tablespoons cooking oil

¼   pound mild or hot sausages, casings removed

2   onions, chopped

3   cloves garlic, minced

1   pound kale, tough stems removed, leaves washed well and shredded (about 1½ quarts)

3⅓   cups canned diced tomatoes with their juice (two 15-ounce cans)

1¼   teaspoons salt

½   teaspoon fresh-ground black pepper

4   cups drained and rinsed canned cannellini beans (two 19-ounce cans)

1.   In a Dutch oven, heat 1 tablespoon of the oil over moderate heat. Add the sausage and cook, breaking the meat up with a fork, until it loses its pink color, about 2 minutes.

Add the remaining tablespoon of oil to the pan and then stir in the onions. Cook, stirring occasionally, until the onions start to soften, about 3 minutes.

2.   Add the garlic and kale to the pan and cook, stirring, until the kale wilts, about 2 minutes. Stir in the tomatoes, salt, and pepper; bring to a simmer. Reduce the heat and simmer, covered, until the kale is tender, about 15 minutes.

3.   Stir the beans into the stew and cook until warmed through, about 5 minutes. If you like, mash some of the beans with a fork to thicken the sauce.

VEGETABLE TIP

Shred **kale** leaves as fine as possible when making quick soups and stews, so that each bite will include tender greens instead of a chewy mouthful.

SQUASH, BEAN, AND CORN STEW

Beans, an essential part of the South American diet, join other staples from that part of the world—corn, squash, and tomatoes—in this extremely popular Chilean vegetable stew. We've chosen kidney beans, but you can use pinto, cannellini, or any type you have on hand.

WINE RECOMMENDATION
Gewurztraminers from Alsace have a unique combination of aromas: rose petals, ripe apricots, and musky spice. Though called dry, these wines usually contain a bit of residual sugar—a real plus for this dish, with its sweet squash and corn.

SERVES 4

¼ cup olive oil

2 onions, sliced thin

2 cloves garlic, chopped

½ teaspoon paprika

¼ teaspoon cayenne

1 teaspoon dried oregano

2 tablespoons drained chopped pimientos (one 4-ounce jar)

1 cup canned crushed tomatoes in thick puree (from a 15-ounce can)

1 butternut squash (about 2 pounds), peeled, halved lengthwise, seeded, and cut into 1-inch dice

1½ cups water

2 teaspoons salt

2 cups drained and rinsed canned kidney beans (one 19-ounce can)

2 cups fresh (cut from about 4 ears) or frozen corn kernels

½ cup chopped fresh basil (optional)

1. In a Dutch oven, heat the oil over moderately low heat. Add the onions and cook, stirring occasionally, until translucent, about 5 minutes. Add the garlic, paprika, cayenne, and oregano and cook, stirring, until fragrant, about 1 minute.

2. Stir in the pimientos, tomatoes, squash, water, and salt and bring to a simmer. Cook the stew, covered, stirring occasionally, until the squash is almost tender, about 15 minutes. Uncover and simmer vigorously until almost no liquid remains in the pan, about 5 minutes. Add the beans and corn and cook until the corn is just tender, about 5 minutes. Stir in the basil.

VARIATIONS

■ Add one cup of diced **ham** along with the beans and corn.
■ Use peeled, cubed **pumpkin** or **acorn squash** instead of the butternut squash.

BUTTERNUT-SQUASH COUSCOUS

The word *couscous* refers to both the tiny semolina pearls themselves and to the dish of couscous topped with a hearty stew, just as other types of pasta are *pasta* whether dressed with a sauce or not. Here, butternut squash substitutes for the pumpkin more commonly found in North Africa.

WINE RECOMMENDATION
For the best effect, look for a soft, fruity red wine to contrast with the spicy flavors of the couscous. The plummy flavor and supple texture of a rich California merlot will make a terrific match.

SERVES 4

¼ cup sliced almonds

2 tablespoons olive oil

2 onions, chopped

2 cloves garlic, minced

¼ teaspoon cayenne

⅛ teaspoon grated nutmeg

⅛ teaspoon cinnamon

1 cup canned diced tomatoes with their juice (from one 15-ounce can)

1 butternut squash (about 2 pounds), peeled, halved lengthwise, seeded, and cut into ¾-inch dice

¼ cup raisins

3 cups canned low-sodium chicken broth or homemade stock

1¼ teaspoons salt

2 cups drained and rinsed canned chickpeas (one 19-ounce can)

¾ cup chopped fresh parsley

1½ cups water

1½ cups couscous

1. In a small frying pan, toast the almonds over moderately low heat, stirring frequently, until golden brown, about 5 minutes. Or, toast them in a 350° oven for 5 to 10 minutes.

2. In a Dutch oven, heat the oil over moderately low heat. Add the onions and cook, stirring occasionally, until translucent, about 5 minutes. Add the garlic, cayenne, nutmeg, and cinnamon and cook, stirring, until fragrant, 1 minute longer. Stir in the tomatoes, squash, raisins, broth, and 1 teaspoon of the salt and bring to a simmer. Stir in the chickpeas and cook, covered, for 10 minutes. Uncover and simmer until the squash is tender, about 10 minutes more. Stir in the parsley.

3. Meanwhile, in a medium saucepan, bring the water and the remaining ¼ teaspoon salt to a boil. Stir in the couscous. Cover, remove from the heat, and let stand for 5 minutes. Fluff with a fork. Serve the stew over the couscous and top with the toasted almonds.

SWISS-CHARD, POTATO, AND CHICKPEA STEW

Inspired by the full-flavored vegetable stews of Spain, this earthy fare satisfies the stomach and warms the soul. Don't worry if some of the potato slices break up during cooking; they'll just add to the country feeling.

WINE RECOMMENDATION
A cozy cold-weather stew, with its earth-bound flavors, begs for a similarly rustic, full-bodied white wine. A white Côtes-du-Rhône from the warm and sunny south of France will fill the bill nicely.

SERVES 4

1 pound Swiss chard, tough stems removed, leaves washed well and chopped

3 tablespoons olive oil

1½ pounds baking potatoes (about 3), peeled and sliced ¾-inch thick

1 onion, chopped

2 cloves garlic, minced

1 teaspoon paprika

¼ teaspoon turmeric

⅛ teaspoon cayenne

1 teaspoon salt

2 cups drained and rinsed canned chickpeas (one 19-ounce can)

3 cups canned low-sodium chicken broth or homemade stock

1 cup water

2 hard-cooked eggs, cut into wedges

1. Bring a medium pot of salted water to a boil. Add the chard and cook for 3 minutes. Drain thoroughly and set aside.

2. In a Dutch oven, heat the oil over moderate heat. Add the potatoes and onion and sauté, stirring frequently, until the potatoes start to brown, about 5 minutes. Add the garlic, paprika, turmeric, cayenne, and salt and cook, stirring, until fragrant, about 1 minute.

3. Add the cooked chard, chickpeas, broth, and water. Bring to a simmer and cook until the potatoes are tender, about 15 minutes. Serve the stew garnished with the hard-cooked eggs.

VEGETABLE TIP

Swiss chard is available with either reddish or light-green stalks. The red variety has a slightly stronger flavor, but the two are generally interchangeable.

WINTER-VEGETABLE SHEPHERD'S PIE

You have considerable leeway in assembling the ingredients for this English-inspired meal in a dish, but there should always be carrots, onions, and at least three other vegetables, one of them green. Leftover mashed potatoes work fine to top the vegetable stew, which can be browned under the broiler or in a hot oven.

WINE RECOMMENDATION

Merlot has become so much of a cliché that we tend to shy away from it, but this dish will definitely profit from a juicy merlot from the south of France.

SERVES 4

- 2 pounds baking potatoes (about 4), peeled and cut into large pieces
- 1½ teaspoons salt
- ¾ teaspoon fresh-ground black pepper
- 1 cup heavy cream
- 6 tablespoons butter
- 2 large onions, sliced
- 1 clove garlic, minced
- 4 cups sliced mixed winter vegetables, such as celery, turnips, Brussels sprouts, parsnips, fennel, cabbage, or celery root
- 2 carrots, sliced
- ¼ teaspoon dried thyme
- 3 cups canned low-sodium chicken broth or homemade stock

1. Put the potatoes in a medium saucepan of salted water. Bring to a boil, reduce the heat, and simmer until the potatoes are tender, about 15 minutes. Drain the potatoes and put them back into the saucepan along with 1 teaspoon of the salt and ¼ teaspoon of the pepper. Mash the potatoes over very low heat, gradually incorporating the cream and 4 tablespoons of the butter. Cover and set aside.

2. Meanwhile, in a Dutch oven, melt the remaining 2 tablespoons of butter over moderately low heat. Add the onions and cook, stirring occasionally, until golden, about 10 minutes. Add the garlic and cook, stirring, until fragrant, about 1 minute. Stir in the sliced mixed vegetables, carrots, thyme, and the remaining ½ teaspoon each of salt and pepper. Mix well.

3. Stir in the broth and bring to a simmer. Cook over moderate heat, covered, until the vegetables start to soften, 5 to 10 minutes. Uncover, increase the heat to moderately high, and cook until the vegetables are tender and almost no liquid remains in the pan, about 10 minutes longer.

4. Heat the broiler. Transfer the vegetables to a 9-inch pie plate, spread the potatoes over the top, and cook until lightly browned, about 5 minutes.

OKRA AND GREEN-PEA CURRY

Americans are not overly fond of okra; outside of the South, it's rarely eaten and rarely missed. In India, though, okra is much beloved and is prepared in many ways: fried, stuffed, and, as here, braised briefly with tomatoes and onions. We promise that our method will *not* give you a slimy vegetable, just barely tender okra with great flavor. Serve the curry over rice with a little plain yogurt.

WINE RECOMMENDATION

It's been said that gewurztraminer is the best match for curry, and we won't disagree. Try one from Alsace for its power and depth of flavor.

SERVES 4

3 tablespoons cooking oil

2 onions, sliced

2 cloves garlic, minced

1 tablespoon grated fresh ginger

1 teaspoon fennel seeds

½ teaspoon ground coriander

½ teaspoon ground cumin

½ teaspoon turmeric

¼ teaspoon cayenne

1 cup canned diced tomatoes with their juice (from one 15-ounce can)

2 10-ounce packages frozen cut okra, defrosted

1 10-ounce package frozen peas

½ cup water

2¾ teaspoons salt

1 tablespoon lemon juice

½ cup chopped cilantro

1. In a Dutch oven, heat the oil over moderately low heat. Add the onions and cook, stirring occasionally, until translucent, about 5 minutes. Add the garlic and ginger and cook, stirring, until fragrant, about 1 minute. Stir in the fennel seeds, coriander, cumin, turmeric, and cayenne and cook, stirring, for 1 minute longer. Increase the heat to moderate. Add the tomatoes and cook, stirring frequently, until no liquid remains in the pan, about 5 minutes.

2. Add the okra, peas, water, and salt and simmer just until the vegetables are tender, 3 to 5 minutes. Stir in the lemon juice and cilantro.

VEGETABLE TIP

Since perfectly fresh, sweet **peas** are so hard to find, frozen peas are almost always an acceptable substitute. In fact, frozen peas are generally of such high quality, we rate them as our favorite frozen vegetable.

EGGPLANT AND POTATO CURRY

Charring the eggplant before cooking is well worth the little bit of extra time it takes; it gives the whole dish an enticing smokiness. Serve the curry with rice (preferably basmati) and, if you like, top with additional chopped cilantro and tomatoes.

WINE RECOMMENDATION
A robust, grenache-based Gigondas or Vacqueyras from the southern Rhône valley will meld beautifully with the smoky and earthy flavors of this curry.

SERVES 4

- 2 large eggplants (about 1½ pounds each), pricked all over with a fork
- 3 tablespoons cooking oil
- 2 onions, sliced
- 2 cloves garlic, minced
- 2 tablespoons grated fresh ginger
- ½ teaspoon ground coriander
- ½ teaspoon ground cumin
- 1 teaspoon fennel seeds
- 1 jalapeño pepper, seeds and ribs removed, minced
- 1 pound baking potatoes (about 2), peeled and cut into ½-inch cubes
- 2 teaspoons salt
- 2 cups water
- 3 medium tomatoes (about 1 pound), chopped
- 2 tablespoons lemon juice
- ½ cup chopped cilantro

1. Heat the broiler. Put the whole eggplants on a baking sheet and broil, turning occasionally, until charred and soft, about 10 minutes. Set aside to cool.

2. In a Dutch oven, heat the oil over moderately low heat. Add the onions and cook, stirring occasionally, until translucent, about 5 minutes. Add the garlic and ginger and cook, stirring, until fragrant, about 1 minute. Stir in the coriander, cumin, fennel seeds, and jalapeño and cook, stirring, for 1 minute longer. Add the potatoes, salt, and water and bring to a simmer. Cook, covered, until the potatoes start to soften, about 10 minutes.

3. Cut each eggplant open and spoon the pulp into the potato mixture. Simmer, uncovered, until the potatoes are tender, about 5 minutes more. Add the tomatoes and heat through, about 2 minutes. Stir in the lemon juice and cilantro.

THAI VEGETABLE CURRY

Green curry paste can be pretty fiery. If that's appealing to you, lay it on! If not, use just a little, or try red or yellow curry paste instead. These are somewhat milder—though in no way bland—and they're becoming more and more available in the Asian section of supermarkets. Serve the curry with steamed jasmine or regular white rice.

WINE RECOMMENDATION
An off-dry gewurztraminer from the Pacific Northwest is a good choice to both accentuate the curry spice flavors and tame their heat.

SERVES 4

1½ tablespoons cooking oil

1 onion, sliced thin

1 to 1½ teaspoons Thai green curry paste

1⅔ cups canned unsweetened coconut milk (one 15-ounce can)

1 cup canned low-sodium chicken broth or homemade stock

1½ tablespoons soy sauce

1 teaspoon brown sugar

1 teaspoon salt

⅓ cup drained canned bamboo shoots, halved

1 pound boiling potatoes (about 2), peeled and cut into 1-inch cubes

1 pound broccoli, thick stems removed, tops cut into small florets (1 quart)

1 tomato, chopped

1½ teaspoons lime juice

⅓ cup thin-sliced basil leaves

1. In a Dutch oven, heat the oil over moderate heat. Add the onion and cook, stirring occasionally, until starting to soften, about 3 minutes. Stir in the curry paste and fry, stirring, for 1 minute.

2. Add the coconut milk and broth and bring to a boil. Stir in the soy sauce, brown sugar, salt, bamboo shoots, potatoes, and broccoli. Reduce the heat and simmer, partially covered, until the vegetables are tender, about 10 minutes.

3. Stir in the tomato and heat through, about 2 minutes. Remove from the heat and add the lime juice and basil.

VARIATIONS

Other vegetables that would taste good in place of the broccoli include **carrots**, **eggplant**, **cauliflower**, **snow peas**, **cabbage**, **green beans**, and **canned baby corn**. Try your favorite, or use a combination of vegetables.

CHAPTER TWO

Pasta

FETTUCCINE WITH CHERRY TOMATOES AND WATERCRESS

Succulent little cherry tomatoes know no season, so you can enjoy this fresh-tasting no-cook pasta sauce any time of year. Marinate the tomatoes for at least the time it takes to boil the water and cook the fettuccine; the longer you let them sit, the better the sauce will taste.

WINE RECOMMENDATION
With its fresh tomatoes and peppery watercress, this pasta requires a crisp, light red to bring out its best. See if you can find a rosé-like grignolino from the Piedmont region of Italy. If not, a Valpolicella or Bardolino, both from the Veneto, will do nicely.

SERVES 4

1½ pounds cherry tomatoes, quartered (about 1 quart)

2 cloves garlic, smashed

6 tablespoons olive oil

¾ teaspoon salt

¼ teaspoon fresh-ground black pepper

½ cup thin-sliced basil leaves or chopped fresh parsley

¾ pound fettuccine

2 bunches watercress (about 10 ounces in all), tough stems removed (about 5 cups)

1. In a large glass or stainless-steel bowl, toss the tomatoes with the garlic, oil, ½ teaspoon of the salt, the pepper, and basil. Set the mixture aside.

2. In a large pot of boiling, salted water, cook the fettuccine until just done, about 12 minutes. Drain, return to the hot pan, and toss with the tomato mixture, the watercress, and the remaining ¼ teaspoon salt.

VARIATIONS

■ Use five cups of shredded **arugula** leaves instead of the watercress.
■ If you have lovely ripe summer **tomatoes**, substitute them for the cherry tomatoes.
■ For a more colorful version, use **spinach fettuccine** instead of regular. The taste will be just slightly different.
■ Serve the pasta with a little bit of **goat cheese** crumbled over the top.

SPAGHETTINI WITH ONIONS, SCALLIONS, AND GARLIC

Supporting players become stars in a simple spaghettini recipe that gives onions, scallions, and garlic a chance to shine. Other members of the lily family—leeks, shallots, chives—make good understudies; use them as additions or substitutions.

WINE RECOMMENDATION
There are no tomatoes in this sauce, but you'll still want a red wine—the rich Parmesan needs the tannins to provide balance. Go for a basic (not Riserva) Chianti and enjoy its bright, slightly bitter-cherry and earth flavors.

SERVES 4

¼ pound sliced bacon, cut crosswise into ½-inch strips

2 large onions, sliced thin

½ teaspoon salt

6 scallions, white bulbs cut into ½-inch lengths, green tops chopped

4 cloves garlic, sliced thin

1¾ cups canned low-sodium chicken broth or homemade stock

¾ pound spaghettini

½ cup grated Parmesan

1. In a large deep frying pan, cook the bacon over moderate heat until crisp. Remove the bacon with a slotted spoon. Pour off all but 3 tablespoons of the bacon fat or, if you don't have 3 tablespoons, add enough olive oil to make up the amount. Put the pan over moderately low heat. Add the onions and ¼ teaspoon of the salt. Cook, covered, for 5 minutes.

2. Uncover the pan and continue cooking, stirring occasionally, until the onions are golden, 10 to 15 minutes. Stir in the scallion bulbs and the garlic; cook 2 minutes longer, stirring occasionally. Add the broth and bring to a simmer.

3. Meanwhile, in a large pot of boiling, salted water, cook the spaghettini until almost done, about 9 minutes. Drain the spaghettini and add it to the simmering broth. Cook until the pasta is just done, about 3 minutes. Stir in the Parmesan and the remaining ¼ teaspoon salt. Toss with the bacon and scallion greens.

VEGETABLE TIP

Scallions, also known as green onions, are essentially an herb and a vegetable in one. The bulbs can be used like a regular onion, while the green tops make a great flavoring and garnish. In fact, the chopped tops can be used as a substitute for chives.

LINGUINE WITH SNOW PEAS, CUCUMBER, AND PEANUT SAUCE

Kids will be especially fond of this Asian-inspired noodle dish—after all, the sauce is made with peanut butter—but the combination of cooked and raw vegetables is refreshing and satisfying enough to please all ages. Serve the pasta immediately after tossing it with the peanut mixture; the sauce gets thick if it sits too long.

WINE RECOMMENDATION
Choose a simple kabinett riesling from the Rheinhessen. These rieslings' piquant juxtaposition of fruity acids and balancing sweetness is the perfect foil for the salty and spicy flavors of Asian cuisine.

SERVES 4

- 2   cloves garlic
- 2   tablespoons soy sauce
- ⅓   cup peanut butter
- ⅔   cup canned low-sodium chicken broth or homemade stock
- 1½ tablespoons lime juice
- ½   teaspoon red-pepper flakes
- ¾   teaspoon salt
- ¾   pound linguine
- ½   pound snow peas, cut diagonally into thin slices
- 1½ cups bean sprouts (about ¼ pound)
- 2   scallions including green tops, chopped
- 1   cucumber, peeled, halved lengthwise, seeded, and sliced thin
- ½   cup chopped peanuts

1. In a blender or food processor, combine the garlic, soy sauce, peanut butter, chicken broth, lime juice, red-pepper flakes, and ½ teaspoon of the salt. Puree until smooth.

2. In a large pot of boiling, salted water, cook the linguine until almost done, about 9 minutes. Stir in the snow peas and bean sprouts and cook until the vegetables and pasta are just done, about 3 minutes more. Drain and toss with the peanut sauce, the remaining ¼ teaspoon salt, the scallions, cucumber, and ⅓ cup of the peanuts. Serve with the remaining peanuts sprinkled over the top.

VEGETABLE TIP

Though they're certainly edible, the seeds from a mature **cucumber** can be somewhat watery. You can simply scoop them out of a halved cucumber with a spoon and discard them—or buy an English (hothouse) cucumber, which is almost completely seedless.

PENNE SALAD WITH EGGPLANT

Unlike some pasta salads, this one is best served at room temperature. Don't refrigerate it, or the penne will get gummy and unpleasant. We've peeled the eggplant here, but if you like the texture of eggplant skin, leave it on.

WINE RECOMMENDATION

Chianti is one of the versatility champions of the wine world. Its high acidity, medium body, moderate tannins, and understated dried-cherry fruit allow it to play a supporting role with many cuisines. Serve one here and you'll see why.

SERVES 4

8 tablespoons olive oil

1 large eggplant (about 1¾ pounds), peeled and cut into ½-inch cubes

1¼ teaspoons salt

2 cloves garlic, minced

¾ pound penne

½ cup chopped fresh parsley

¼ teaspoon fresh-ground black pepper

2 tablespoons lemon juice

1. In a large nonstick frying pan, heat 2 tablespoons of the oil over moderate heat. Add one third of the eggplant and ¼ teaspoon of the salt and cook, stirring occasionally, until the eggplant is tender and brown, about 4 minutes. Remove the eggplant from the pan and put it in a large bowl. Cook the remaining eggplant in two batches, each using 2 tablespoons of the oil and ¼ teaspoon of the salt. Add the garlic to the last batch of eggplant during the final minute of cooking.

2. Meanwhile, in a large pot of boiling, salted water, cook the penne until just done, about 13 minutes. Drain. Rinse with cold water and drain thoroughly. Transfer to the bowl with the eggplant.

3. Toss the pasta and eggplant with the remaining 2 tablespoons oil and ½ teaspoon salt, the parsley, pepper, and lemon juice.

VEGETABLE TIP

Eggplant soaks up oil like a sponge; so it's best to cook this vegetable in a nonstick pan. That way, you can limit the amount of oil available for the eggplant to absorb without worrying about it sticking.

LINGUINE WITH MOM'S EGGPLANT-AND-MUSHROOM SAUCE

It's spaghetti sauce like Mom used to make, but without the hours and hours of simmering. Our version, chunky with bits of eggplant and mushrooms, is just a bit more sophisticated but every bit as satisfying.

WINE RECOMMENDATION
Pasta almost always brings us back to Italy and her bountiful variety of wines. A Dolcetto d'Alba, light and fruity but with firm tannins, is what you want to perfectly offset the traditional flavors and high acidity of the sauce.

SERVES 4

3 tablespoons olive oil

1 onion, chopped

½ pound mushrooms, coarsely chopped

1 eggplant, peeled and cut into ½-inch cubes

1¼ teaspoons salt

⅛ teaspoon cayenne

¾ teaspoon dried thyme

1¾ cups canned crushed tomatoes in thick puree (one 15-ounce can)

½ cup canned low-sodium chicken broth or homemade stock

¾ pound linguine

1. In a large nonstick frying pan, heat 1 tablespoon of the oil over moderately low heat. Add the onion and cook, stirring occasionally, until the onion is translucent, about 5 minutes. Increase the heat to moderately high and add another tablespoon of the oil to the pan. Add the mushrooms and cook, stirring, until golden brown, 3 to 5 minutes.

2. Reduce the heat to moderate. Add the remaining tablespoon of oil to the pan. Stir in the eggplant and cook, stirring occasionally, for 5 minutes. Add the salt, cayenne, thyme, tomatoes, and broth. Bring to a simmer. Reduce the heat and simmer, covered, until the eggplant is very tender, about 30 minutes.

3. Meanwhile, in a large pot of boiling, salted water, cook the linguine until just done, about 12 minutes. Drain; toss with the sauce.

VEGETABLE TIP

When sautéing **mushrooms**, cook them over relatively high heat and in batches to avoid overcrowding the pan. If the heat's too low or the pan too full, the mushrooms will steam in their own liquid instead of browning. It's worth the extra effort to avoid that rubbery, steamed texture—unless you're especially fond of *canned* mushrooms.

FETTUCCINE WITH MUSHROOMS, TARRAGON, AND GOAT-CHEESE SAUCE

The delectably rich-tasting sauce that clings to each strand of fettuccine here requires no cooking. Just combine goat cheese, Parmesan, milk, and some of the still-hot pasta-cooking water, and it's done.

WINE RECOMMENDATION
Dolcetto, while beloved in Piedmont, is less appreciated in the United States. Yet its light tannins, cherry fruit, and clean, dry finish are just the ticket to balance the full flavor of the cheeses here.

SERVES 4

- 1 tablespoon butter
- 2 tablespoons olive oil
- 1 pound mushrooms, cut into thin slices
- 1 teaspoon salt
- ¼ teaspoon fresh-ground black pepper
- 2 tablespoons chopped fresh tarragon, or 2 teaspoons dried tarragon
- ½ pound mild goat cheese
- ⅓ cup grated Parmesan, plus more for serving
- ⅓ cup milk
- ¾ pound fettuccine
- 2 tablespoons chopped fresh chives or scallion tops

1. In a large frying pan, melt the butter with 1 tablespoon of the oil over high heat. Add the mushrooms, ½ teaspoon of the salt, the pepper, and the dried tarragon, if using, and cook, stirring, for 3 minutes. Reduce the heat to moderately high and continue cooking, stirring occasionally, until the mushrooms are golden brown and no liquid remains in the pan, about 5 minutes.

2. In a small bowl, combine the goat cheese, Parmesan, milk, and ¼ teaspoon of the salt. Stir until smooth.

3. Meanwhile, in a large pot of boiling, salted water, cook the fettuccine until just done, about 12 minutes. Reserve 1½ cups of the pasta-cooking water and drain. Whisk 1 cup of the pasta-cooking water into the goat-cheese mixture. Toss the pasta with the mushrooms, the goat-cheese sauce, the remaining ¼ teaspoon salt and 1 tablespoon olive oil, the fresh tarragon, if using, and the chives. If the pasta seems dry, add more of the reserved pasta-cooking water. Serve with additional Parmesan.

VARIATION

Use fresh **basil** instead of or in addition to the tarragon and chives in the recipe.

SPAGHETTI WITH ESCAROLE AND BACON

Crisp bacon complements escarole so well that you may be tempted to sauté the greens in the bacon fat, but don't do it; the bacon will then overwhelm the greens completely. Use olive oil instead, which will bring all the flavors together.

 WINE RECOMMENDATION
Italian white wines were made for dishes like this one. Soave, Orvieto, Frascati—all are based on the trebbiano grape and have the crisp, neutral, refreshing taste and light body that allow the pasta to take center stage.

SERVES 4

¼ pound sliced bacon, cut crosswise into thin strips

2 tablespoons olive oil

3 cloves garlic, minced

¼ teaspoon red-pepper flakes

1½ teaspoons anchovy paste

1 head escarole (about 1½ pounds), leaves cut into ½-inch strips (about 3 quarts)

⅔ cup canned low-sodium chicken broth or homemade stock

½ teaspoon salt

¾ pound spaghetti

⅓ cup grated Parmesan, plus more for serving

1 tablespoon butter

1. In a large deep frying pan, cook the bacon over moderate heat until crisp. Remove the bacon with a slotted spoon. Pour off all the fat from the pan.

2. In the same pan, heat the oil over moderately low heat. Add the garlic, red-pepper flakes, and anchovy paste and cook, stirring, until fragrant, about 30 seconds. Stir in the escarole, a little at a time, until wilted, about 3 minutes. Add the broth and ¼ teaspoon of the salt and bring to a simmer. Reduce the heat and cook, covered, for 5 minutes.

3. Meanwhile, in a large pot of boiling, salted water, cook the spaghetti until just done, about 12 minutes. Drain the pasta; add it to the pan with the escarole. Stir in the remaining ¼ teaspoon salt, the Parmesan, bacon, and butter.

VARIATIONS

■ Stir in a cup of drained canned **cannellini beans** when you add the broth in Step 2.
■ Add two tablespoons of chopped fresh **basil** just before serving.

ORECCHIETTE WITH BROCCOLI AND TOMATOES

Balsamic vinegar adds a hint of sweetness to this savory sauce. If the slight sweet-and-sour effect isn't to your taste, either omit the vinegar completely or use wine vinegar instead. The effect will be different, but no less delicious.

WINE RECOMMENDATION
With its tomato-and-vinegar based sauce, this pasta cries out for a light, tart Italian red such as Valpolicella. The wine's crisp cherry flavor will act as a perfect foil for this dish.

SERVES 4

3   tablespoons olive oil

2   cloves garlic, minced

1½ pounds broccoli, thick stems peeled, halved lengthwise, and cut into ½-inch pieces, tops cut into small florets (about 1½ quarts in all)

1   teaspoon salt

¼   teaspoon fresh-ground black pepper

1⅔ cups canned diced tomatoes with their juice (one 15-ounce can)

¼   cup canned low-sodium chicken broth or homemade stock

¾   pound orecchiette

1   teaspoon balsamic vinegar

⅓   cup chopped fresh parsley

2   tablespoons butter

1. In a large deep frying pan, heat the oil over moderately low heat. Add the garlic and broccoli stems and cook, stirring occasionally, for 2 minutes. Add the broccoli florets, ½ teaspoon of the salt, and the pepper. Stir to coat with the oil.

2. Add the tomatoes and broth to the broccoli and bring to a simmer. Reduce the heat and simmer, covered, until the broccoli is tender, 5 to 10 minutes.

3. Meanwhile, in a large pot of boiling, salted water, cook the orecchiette until done, about 15 minutes. Drain the pasta and add it to the pan with the broccoli. Remove the pan from the heat. Add the vinegar, the remaining ½ teaspoon salt, the parsley, and butter. Stir gently until the butter just coats the pasta.

VEGETABLE TIP

Broccoli stems are a delicious vegetable in their own right. Peel the thick skin and then slice or cut the stems into pieces. If you're cooking them with the florets, either cut the stems into quite small pieces so they'll be done at the same time, or cook them for a few minutes before adding the florets.

RIGATONI WITH CAULIFLOWER AND TOMATO SAUCE

Even if you've never been particularly fond of cauliflower, we think you'll find this pasta pretty irresistible. The vegetable is braised with garlic, sweet raisins, and crushed tomatoes until tender and then tossed with crunchy toasted pine nuts and chunky rigatoni. What's not to love?

WINE RECOMMENDATION
Barbera is the everyday wine of the Piedmontese, and this pasta will show you why. High in acid, low in tannin, and chock-full of bright blackberry fruitiness, barberas are perhaps the best wines in the world to serve with tomato-based dishes.

SERVES 4

1/3 cup pine nuts

3 tablespoons olive oil

3 cloves garlic, minced

1 small head cauliflower (about 1½ pounds), cut into small florets (about 1 quart florets)

1¾ cups canned crushed tomatoes in thick puree (one 15-ounce can)

1/3 cup raisins

2 tablespoons water

¾ teaspoon salt

¾ pound rigatoni

½ cup thin-sliced basil leaves or chopped fresh parsley

¼ cup grated Parmesan, plus more for serving

¼ teaspoon fresh-ground black pepper

1. In a small frying pan, toast the pine nuts over moderately low heat, stirring frequently, until golden brown, about 5 minutes. Or toast them in a 350° oven for 5 to 10 minutes.

2. In a large frying pan, heat the oil over moderately low heat. Add the garlic and cook until fragrant, stirring, about 30 seconds. Increase the heat to moderate. Add the cauliflower, tomatoes, raisins, water, and salt and bring the sauce to a simmer. Reduce the heat and simmer, covered, until the cauliflower is very tender, about 10 minutes.

3. In a large pot of boiling, salted water, cook the rigatoni until just done, about 14 minutes. Drain the rigatoni and toss with the pine nuts, cauliflower sauce, basil, Parmesan, and pepper. Serve with additional Parmesan.

PENNE WITH ROASTED BUTTERNUT SQUASH AND HAM

Soft and creamy mascarpone cheese forms the base for a pasta sauce that's deliciously rich and absolutely simple. This dish also makes a fabulous first course for six.

 WINE RECOMMENDATION
A gewurztraminer from Alsace may sound like an unusual choice here, but try it; you'll be surprised at how beautifully the sweet butternut squash and salty ham blend with the wine's rich, spicy flavors.

SERVES 4

1 butternut squash (about 2 pounds), peeled, halved lengthwise, seeded, and cut into ½-inch dice

2 tablespoons olive oil

1 teaspoon salt

⅛ teaspoon fresh-ground black pepper

1¼ teaspoons dried sage

1 cup mascarpone cheese

½ cup half-and-half

3 scallions including green tops, chopped

¾ pound penne

¼ pound sliced smoked ham, such as Black Forest, cut into thin strips

¼ cup grated Parmesan

1. Heat the oven to 450°. Put the squash on a large baking sheet and toss with the oil, ¼ teaspoon of the salt, the pepper, and sage. Spread the squash out in a single layer. Roast, turning occasionally, until tender and starting to brown, 15 to 20 minutes.

2. In a small bowl, stir together the mascarpone, half-and-half, scallions, and the remaining ¾ teaspoon salt.

3. Meanwhile, in a large pot of boiling, salted water, cook the penne until just done, about 13 minutes. Reserve 1 cup of the pasta-cooking water and drain. Return the pasta to the hot pan. Stir in the squash, mascarpone sauce, and ham. If the sauce seems too thick, add some of the reserved pasta-cooking water. Serve topped with the Parmesan.

VARIATIONS

Instead of butternut squash, roast cubes of another winter squash, such as **pumpkin** or **acorn squash**—or try roasting cubed **sweet potatoes**.

Pumpkin Lasagne

No need to roast fresh pumpkin for this dish (although you certainly *could*); using canned unseasoned pumpkin puree is much quicker, and it works just fine. Like most lasagnes, this one is easier to cut if left to set for ten minutes or so before serving.

WINE RECOMMENDATION
The sweet pumpkin and rich Parmesan require a powerful white with some sweetness of its own. An Oregon pinot gris will be perfect.

SERVES 4

- 2 tablespoons olive oil
- 2 onions, chopped
- 2 pounds Swiss chard, tough stems removed, leaves washed well and chopped
- 2¼ teaspoons salt
- 1 teaspoon fresh-ground black pepper
- 1 teaspoon dried sage
- ½ teaspoon grated nutmeg
- 3 cups canned pumpkin puree (one 28-ounce can)
- 1½ cups heavy cream
- 1½ cups grated Parmesan
- ½ cup milk
- 9 no-boil lasagne noodles (about 6 ounces)
- 1 tablespoon butter

1. In a large nonstick frying pan, heat the oil over moderately low heat. Add the onions and cook, stirring occasionally, until translucent, about 5 minutes. Increase the heat to moderately high and add the chard, 1 teaspoon salt, ½ teaspoon pepper, ½ teaspoon sage, and ¼ teaspoon nutmeg. Cook, stirring, until the chard is wilted and no liquid remains in the pan, 5 to 10 minutes.

2. Heat the oven to 400°. In a medium bowl, mix together 2 cups of the pumpkin, ¾ cup cream, ½ cup Parmesan, and the remaining 1¼ teaspoons salt, ½ teaspoon pepper, ½ teaspoon sage, and ¼ teaspoon nutmeg.

3. Pour the milk into an 8-by-12-inch baking dish. Top the milk with one third of the noodles, then spread half the pumpkin mixture over the noodles. Layer half the Swiss chard over the pumpkin and top with a second layer of noodles. Repeat with another layer of pumpkin, Swiss chard, and noodles. Combine the remaining 1 cup of pumpkin and ¾ cup of cream. Spread the mixture evenly over the top of the lasagne, sprinkle with the remaining 1 cup of Parmesan, and dot with the butter. Cover with aluminum foil and bake for 20 minutes. Uncover and bake until golden, about 15 minutes more.

RAVIOLI NUDI IN TOMATO SAUCE

Hear the name *ravioli nudi*—literally, *naked ravioli*—and you may envision little sauce-less pasta packets, but in fact it's not the sauce that's missing, but the pasta itself. Ravioli filling, in this case spinach and ricotta, is simmered like tender little dumplings. To save time, buy precleaned spinach from the salad bar.

WINE RECOMMENDATION
Tomatoes require a high-acid wine, while earthy spinach is best with one that has bright, uncomplicated fruit. Sounds like barbera, but no oak please.

SERVES 4

- 2 tablespoons olive oil
- 2 onions, chopped
- 2 pounds spinach, stems removed, leaves washed well and chopped
- 1½ teaspoons salt
- 1 clove garlic, minced
- 1⅔ cups tomato puree (one 15-ounce can)
- ½ cup water
- ¼ teaspoon fresh-ground black pepper
- 1 tablespoon butter
- 1 tablespoon chopped fresh basil or parsley
- ¾ cup ricotta
- ¼ cup grated Parmesan
- 2 eggs, beaten to mix
  Grated zest of 1 lemon
- ⅛ teaspoon grated nutmeg
- 1/16 teaspoon cayenne
- 3 tablespoons flour

1. In a large frying pan, heat 1 tablespoon of the oil over moderately low heat. Add half the onions and cook, stirring occasionally, until translucent, about 5 minutes. Increase the heat to moderately high and add the spinach and 1 teaspoon of the salt. Cook, stirring, until no liquid remains in the pan, about 10 minutes. Drain and press all remaining liquid from the spinach.

2. In the same pan, heat the remaining tablespoon of oil over moderately low heat. Add the remaining onion and cook, stirring occasionally, until translucent, about 5 minutes. Add the garlic and cook for 1 minute, stirring. Stir in the tomato puree, water, pepper, and the remaining ½ teaspoon salt. Bring to a simmer and cook, stirring occasionally, for 15 minutes. Stir in the butter and basil and cover to keep warm.

3. Meanwhile, bring a medium pot of salted water to a simmer. In a medium bowl, combine the cooked spinach, ricotta, Parmesan, eggs, lemon zest, nutmeg, cayenne, and flour. Using two tablespoons, drop walnut-size dumplings into the simmering water. Cook until firm, about 3 minutes. Remove with a slotted spoon and drain on paper towels. Serve with the tomato sauce.

Grains

MUSHROOM FRIED RICE

The quickest—and most authentic—way to make this hearty version of a Chinese-restaurant favorite is to start with leftover rice (you'll need about three cups). But even if you start with raw rice, you'll still be ready to eat in well under an hour.

WINE RECOMMENDATION
Salty, sweet, and hot Asian food lends itself as no other cuisine to the fruity piquancy of German rieslings. Try a simple Qualitätswein bestimmter Anbaugebiete (QbA) from the Mosel for best effect.

SERVES 4

1½	cups long-grain rice
3	tablespoons cooking oil
½	pound cremini mushrooms, sliced thin
½	pound shiitake mushrooms, stems removed, caps sliced
½	pound white mushrooms, sliced thin
¼	teaspoon dried red-pepper flakes
1	tablespoon grated fresh ginger
6	scallions including green tops, sliced thin
½	teaspoon salt
¼	cup soy sauce
½	cup frozen peas
1	teaspoon Asian sesame oil

1. Bring a medium pot of salted water to a boil. Stir in the rice and boil until just done, about 10 minutes. Drain the rice and set aside to cool.

2. Meanwhile, in a large nonstick frying pan or wok, heat 1 tablespoon of the cooking oil over moderately high heat. Add half the mushrooms and cook, stirring frequently, until the mushrooms are tender and golden, about 5 minutes. Transfer to a plate. Repeat with the remaining mushrooms and another tablespoon of the cooking oil. Add these mushrooms to the plate.

3. In the same frying pan, heat the remaining tablespoon of cooking oil over moderate heat. Add the red-pepper flakes, ginger, and scallions and cook, stirring, until fragrant, about 30 seconds. Increase the heat to moderately high and add the rice, salt, and soy sauce. Cook, stirring, for 2 minutes and then add the peas and mushrooms. Cook, stirring, until everything's warm, another 1 to 2 minutes. Remove the pan from the heat and stir in the sesame oil.

VEGETABLE TIP

Most people throw away **shiitake** stems because they're tough. But you can simmer them gently in stock, or any liquid, until they're tender. If that's too much trouble, just save them to add flavor to stock.

HOPPIN' JOHN

A New Year's Day tradition in many Southern households, this distinctively named dish of rice and black-eyed peas is believed to bring good luck for the coming year. It's often cooked with salt pork; we've substituted smoked sausage, just two ounces per person, but you can leave the meat out altogether if you prefer.

WINE RECOMMENDATION
The robust flavors of Hoppin' John call for an equally assertive wine. Go for a brash, full-bodied red zinfandel from California. Its spicy blackberry richness is easily up to the task.

SERVES 4

3 tablespoons cooking oil

1 onion, chopped

4 scallions, white bulbs sliced and green tops cut into ½-inch pieces

½ pound collard greens, tough stems removed, leaves washed well and shredded

1¾ teaspoons salt

¼ teaspoon fresh-ground black pepper

⅛ teaspoon cayenne

½ pound kielbasa or other smoked sausage, halved lengthwise then cut crosswise into 1-inch slices

1 10-ounce package frozen black-eyed peas

1½ cups long-grain rice

3 cups canned low-sodium chicken broth or homemade stock

1. In a large saucepan or Dutch oven, heat the oil over moderately low heat. Add the onion and the scallion bulbs and cook, stirring occasionally, until the onion is translucent, about 5 minutes. Add the collard greens, salt, black pepper, and cayenne and cook, stirring, until the greens wilt, about 1 minute.

2. Increase the heat to moderately high. Add the sausage, black-eyed peas, and rice and cook, stirring, for 30 seconds. Stir in the broth and bring to a simmer. Reduce the heat to low and cook, covered, until the rice is tender and all the liquid is absorbed, about 20 minutes. Remove from the heat and stir in the scallion tops.

VEGETABLE TIP

Collard greens braised to melting softness in the Southern style (slow-simmered with plenty of pork) are truly delicious, but the greens don't actually have to cook for hours. In twenty minutes they'll be just tender.

VEGETABLE CHILI WITH GARLIC RICE

Here are two recipes for the price of one: a garlicky rice side dish that's also delicious with chicken or shrimp, and a hearty black-bean chili that puts meatier versions to shame. Make enough chili for leftovers; it's even better the next day.

 WINE RECOMMENDATION
A soft and spicy red Côtes-du-Rhône is just the thing for this chili. Its roasted raspberry and herb flavors and light tannins will highlight the various vegetables.

SERVES 4

3 tablespoons cooking oil

1 onion, chopped

5 cloves garlic, minced

1 tablespoon chili powder

2 teaspoons ground cumin

½ teaspoon cayenne

2 red or green bell peppers, cut into ¾-inch squares

1 zucchini, cut into ¾-inch dice

1 yellow squash, cut into ¾-inch dice

1½ teaspoons salt

3½ cups canned diced tomatoes with their juice (two 15-ounce cans)

1⅔ cups drained and rinsed canned black beans (one 15-ounce can)

1½ cups long-grain rice

3 cups canned low-sodium chicken broth or homemade stock

3 tablespoons chopped cilantro (optional)

1. In a large saucepan, heat 2 tablespoons of the oil over moderately low heat. Add the onion and cook, stirring occasionally, until translucent, about 5 minutes. Stir in one third of the garlic, the chili powder, cumin, and cayenne and cook until fragrant, stirring, about 1 minute. Add the bell peppers, zucchini, yellow squash, and 1 teaspoon of the salt. Cook, stirring occasionally, until the vegetables start to soften, about 5 minutes.

2. Add the tomatoes and simmer, stirring occasionally, for 20 minutes. Stir in the beans and simmer until the vegetables are tender, about 5 minutes longer.

3. Meanwhile, in a medium saucepan, heat the remaining tablespoon of oil over moderately low heat. Add the remaining garlic and the rice. Cook, stirring, until the rice is almost opaque, about 2 minutes. Add the broth and the remaining ½ teaspoon of salt and bring to a simmer. Reduce the heat to low and cook, covered, until the rice is tender, about 20 minutes.

4. Stir the cilantro into the chili and serve atop the rice.

VEGETARIAN BIRYANI

The cooks of India and Pakistan take their rice seriously. It is in these regions that the humble grain is transformed into some of southern Asia's most delicious dishes, such as biryani, a richly perfumed combination of rice, vegetables, and sometimes fruits, nuts, and meats. Our vegetarian version features potato, carrots, and peas.

WINE RECOMMENDATION
The sweet, floral perfume of basmati rice calls to mind the similar aromas of Vouvray. A demi-sec will strike just the right balance with the slight heat of the biryani.

SERVES 4

1½ cups rice, preferably basmati, rinsed

1 tablespoon butter

1 tablespoon cooking oil

1 onion, chopped

2 cloves garlic, minced

1 tablespoon grated fresh ginger

½ teaspoon ground cumin

1 teaspoon turmeric

½ teaspoon curry powder

⅛ teaspoon cayenne

1 baking potato (about ½ pound), peeled and cut into 1½-inch pieces

2 carrots, cut into 1½-inch pieces

2 cups water

1½ teaspoons salt

1 10-ounce package frozen peas, defrosted

¼ cup plain yogurt

1 jalapeño pepper, seeds and ribs removed, minced

1 tomato, seeded and cut into ½-inch pieces

½ cup cilantro leaves

1. Bring a medium pot of salted water to a boil. Stir in the rice and boil until just done, about 10 minutes. Drain the rice, return to the pot, and cover to keep warm.

2. Meanwhile, in a large frying pan, melt the butter with the oil over moderately low heat. Add the onion and cook, stirring occasionally, until translucent, about 5 minutes. Add the garlic and ginger and cook, stirring, until fragrant, about 1 minute. Stir in the cumin, turmeric, curry powder, and cayenne and cook, stirring, for 1 minute longer. Add the potato, carrots, water, and salt. Increase the heat to moderately high and simmer until the vegetables are tender and no liquid remains in the pan, about 10 minutes.

3. Stir the peas into the other vegetables and remove the pan from the heat. Stir in the yogurt and rice and serve topped with the jalapeño, tomato, and cilantro.

SPRING-VEGETABLE PAELLA

You don't need a paella pan to make paella; any large frying pan will do. Serve this paella hot or at room temperature (as it is often eaten in Spain), as is or topped with toasted sliced almonds.

WINE RECOMMENDATION
Sauvignon blanc is almost alone in its ability to match both artichokes and asparagus, two normally troubling foods for wines. Pungent, yet balanced, a sauvignon blanc from New Zealand is what you want here.

SERVES 4

2 tablespoons olive oil

1 onion, chopped

¼ cup drained sliced pimientos, chopped (one 4-ounce jar)

1 tomato, peeled and chopped

1 clove garlic, minced

1¼ teaspoons salt

¼ teaspoon turmeric

2 cups rice, preferably medium-grain such as arborio

3 cups canned low-sodium chicken broth or homemade stock

1 cup water

½ cup chopped flat-leaf parsley

½ pound asparagus, tough ends snapped off and discarded, spears cut into 2-inch pieces

1 cup frozen peas

1 6½-ounce jar marinated artichoke hearts, drained and sliced

2 cups drained and rinsed canned cannellini beans (one 19-ounce can)

1. In a large frying pan, heat the oil over moderately low heat. Add the onion and cook, stirring occasionally, until translucent, about 5 minutes. Add the pimientos, tomato, and garlic and cook, stirring occasionally, for 2 minutes.

2. Stir in the salt, turmeric, and rice. Add the chicken broth, water, and parsley and bring to a boil. Continue cooking over moderate heat, stirring frequently, until most of the liquid has been absorbed by the rice, about 7 minutes.

3. Stir in the asparagus, peas, artichokes, and beans. Reduce the heat and simmer, covered, for 15 minutes. Remove from the heat and let stand, covered, for 10 minutes before serving.

SPINACH AND PORCINI-MUSHROOM RISOTTO

The stirring and stirring and stirring for a traditional risotto has a purpose: It releases the starch in the rice, and it's the starch that gives risotto its distinctive creamy texture. We have found, however, that the stirring needn't be constant, just frequent.

WINE RECOMMENDATION
Almost nothing works as well with mushrooms as pinot noir; they were made for each other. One from Oregon will accent fruitiness, while a basic Burgundy, also made from the pinot-noir grape, will be more herbal and earthy. Take your choice.

SERVES 4

½ ounce dried porcini or other dried mushrooms

1 cup boiling water

5 cups canned low-sodium chicken broth or homemade stock, more if needed

3 tablespoons olive oil

1 onion, chopped

2 cups arborio rice

¾ teaspoon salt

⅓ cup dry white wine

¼ cup plus 1 tablespoon cognac or other brandy

½ pound spinach, stems removed, leaves washed well and cut into 1½-inch ribbons

¾ cup grated Parmesan

2 tablespoons butter

1. In a small bowl, soak the dried mushrooms in the boiling water until softened, about 15 minutes. Remove the mushrooms and strain their liquid into a medium saucepan through a sieve lined with a paper towel. Add the broth to the mushroom-soaking liquid; bring to a simmer.

2. Rinse the mushrooms well to remove any grit, chop them, and set aside. In a large pot, heat the oil over moderately low heat. Add the onion and cook, stirring occasionally, until translucent, about 5 minutes. Add the rice and salt and stir until the rice begins to turn opaque, about 2 minutes. Add the wine, the ¼ cup cognac, and the chopped mushrooms. Cook until the liquid has been absorbed.

3. Stir ½ cup of simmering broth into the rice and cook, stirring frequently, until the broth has been absorbed. The rice and the broth should bubble gently; adjust the heat as needed. Continue cooking the rice, adding the broth ½ cup at a time and allowing the rice to absorb the broth before adding the next ½ cup. Cook the rice until almost tender, about 25 minutes, and add the spinach. Cook, stirring, until the rice is tender, about 5 minutes longer. You may not need to use all the liquid, or you may need to add more broth or some water. Stir in the remaining tablespoon of cognac, the Parmesan, and butter.

ESCABÈCHE OF MUSHROOMS WITH POLENTA

In Spain and Mexico, fish and other perishable foods are cooked in a seasoned vinegar mixture; these *escabèche* are then served warm or, more commonly, eaten the next day at room temperature. Though neither mushrooms nor red cabbage can claim to be particularly perishable, they are delicious given the same tangy treatment.

 WINE RECOMMENDATION
Made from tempranillo, Spain's greatest red grape, Riojas offer wonderful concentrated roasted-berry flavors. Long aging in oak barrels gives them a supple, round texture and a complex spiciness that makes them great accompaniment for this *escabèche*.

SERVES 4

6½ cups water

3 teaspoons salt

1⅓ cups coarse or medium cornmeal

2 tablespoons butter

3 tablespoons olive oil

1 red onion, sliced

2 cloves garlic, minced

1 cup canned diced tomatoes with their juice (from one 15-ounce can)

2 tablespoons cider or wine vinegar

1 teaspoon dried oregano

1 jalapeño pepper, seeds and ribs removed, sliced

1 pound mushrooms, sliced

¼ pound shiitake mushrooms, stems removed, caps sliced

½ pound red cabbage (about ¼ head), shredded (about 2 cups)

1 cup chopped cilantro

1. In a medium saucepan, bring 4½ cups of the water and 1 teaspoon of the salt to a boil. Add the cornmeal in a slow stream, whisking. Whisk in the butter. Reduce the heat and simmer, stirring frequently with a wooden spoon, until the polenta is very thick, about 20 minutes. Cover to keep warm.

2. Meanwhile, in a large deep frying pan, heat the oil over moderately low heat. Add the onion and cook, stirring occasionally, until translucent, about 5 minutes. Add the garlic and cook, stirring, for 1 minute. Add the tomatoes, vinegar, oregano, and jalapeño. Cook, stirring frequently, for 5 minutes.

3. Add all the mushrooms, the cabbage, and 1 cup of the water to the pan. Bring to a boil. Cover and reduce the heat to moderately low. Simmer, stirring occasionally, for 15 minutes. Add the remaining 1 cup water and 2 teaspoons salt and simmer, covered, until the vegetables are tender, about 10 minutes more. Stir in the cilantro and serve over the polenta.

BAKED POLENTA WITH MUSHROOMS

In the time it takes to heat up frozen lasagne, you can make a from-scratch layered polenta dish that's every bit as satisfying. It needs nothing more than a simple green salad as an accompaniment.

WINE RECOMMENDATION
To contrast with the cheese here, look for a wine with both good acidity and well-delineated fruit flavors. The earthy red-berry flavors and refreshing tartness of a Bourgogne Rouge, the basic red wine of Burgundy, will be perfect.

SERVES 4

4½ cups water

1½ teaspoons salt

1½ cups coarse or medium cornmeal

3 tablespoons olive oil

¾ teaspoon dried sage

7 tablespoons grated Parmesan

2 tablespoons butter

1½ pounds mushrooms, sliced thin

¼ teaspoon fresh-ground black pepper

6 ounces fontina, grated (about 1½ cups)

1. Heat the oven to 350°. In a medium saucepan, bring the water and 1 teaspoon of the salt to a boil. Add the cornmeal in a slow stream, whisking. Whisk in 1 tablespoon of the oil and ¼ teaspoon of the sage. Reduce the heat and simmer, stirring frequently with a wooden spoon, until very thick, about 20 minutes. Stir in 3 tablespoons of the Parmesan.

2. Meanwhile, butter an 8-by-12-inch baking dish. In a large frying pan, melt 1 tablespoon of the butter with 1 tablespoon of the oil over moderately high heat. Add half the mushrooms, ¼ teaspoon each of the salt and sage, and ⅛ teaspoon of the pepper. Cook, stirring frequently, until the mushrooms are golden, about 5 minutes. Remove. Repeat with the remaining mushrooms, 1 tablespoon each butter and oil, ¼ teaspoon each salt and sage, and ⅛ teaspoon pepper.

3. Pour half the polenta into the baking dish and spread in an even layer. Top with half the mushrooms, followed by half of the fontina and 2 tablespoons of the Parmesan. Repeat with the remaining polenta, mushrooms, fontina, and Parmesan. Bake until the cheese is bubbling, about 15 minutes.

CHEDDAR-CHEESE GRITS WITH SPICY BLACK BEANS

Southern and Southwestern ingredients unite in this sustaining meal of beans, peppers, and tomatoes over the best grits you will ever eat. If you don't have the quick-cooking variety, use regular and follow the instructions on the package.

WINE RECOMMENDATION
The robust and varied flavors in this dish want a big, spicy, and fruity red wine to match their intensity. Zinfandel seems to have an affinity for black beans, and a sturdy example from the Napa Valley will suit these grits and beans well.

SERVES 4

2½ cups water

1 cup milk

2 tablespoons butter

⅛ teaspoon Tabasco sauce

⅛ teaspoon paprika

1¼ teaspoons salt

Cayenne

¾ cup quick-cooking grits

¼ pound cheddar, grated (about 1 cup)

1 red bell pepper, cut into ¾-inch squares

1 green bell pepper, cut into ¾-inch squares

6 scallions including green tops, sliced thin

2 cups drained and rinsed canned black beans (one 19-ounce can)

¼ cup canned low-sodium chicken broth or homemade stock

3 plum tomatoes, chopped

1. In a medium saucepan, combine the water, milk, 1 tablespoon of the butter, the Tabasco, paprika, 1 teaspoon of the salt, and ⅛ teaspoon cayenne. Bring to a boil over moderately high heat. Add the grits in a slow stream, whisking. Reduce the heat, cover, and simmer, stirring frequently with a wooden spoon, until the grits are very thick, 5 to 10 minutes. Remove the saucepan from the heat and stir in the cheese. Cover to keep warm.

2. Meanwhile, in a large nonstick frying pan, melt the remaining tablespoon of butter over moderate heat. Add the bell peppers and scallions and cook, stirring frequently, until the vegetables start to soften, about 5 minutes. Add the beans, broth, ¼ teaspoon cayenne, and the remaining ¼ teaspoon salt. Bring to a simmer and cook, stirring frequently, until the beans are hot, about 5 minutes. Remove from heat and stir in the tomatoes. Serve over the cheese grits.

TABBOULEH WITH TUNA

It seems that every Middle Eastern household has its own version of tabbouleh. Some people prefer the salad made with mostly herbs and greens; others include tomatoes; and some add spices like Aleppo pepper, sumac, and allspice. Our version, made with a little tuna, becomes a main course. Serve it as is or stuffed into pitas.

WINE RECOMMENDATION

This simple dish requires a neutral white wine with high acidity in order not to clash with the mint and to stand up to the lemon juice. An Italian white, such as a pinot bianco from the Alto Adige, ought to fit the bill perfectly.

SERVES 4

1   cup bulgur

2   cups water

6   scallions, white bulbs only, sliced thin

1   cucumber, peeled, halved lengthwise, seeded, and cut into ¼-inch dice

6   radishes, sliced thin

1   carrot, grated

¼   cup chopped fresh parsley

¼   cup chopped fresh mint

1   6-ounce can tuna packed in oil

2   tablespoons olive oil

⅓   cup lemon juice (from 2 lemons)

¾   teaspoon salt

¼   teaspoon fresh-ground black pepper

1. In a small saucepan, combine the bulgur and the water. Bring to a boil over high heat. Reduce the heat to low and cook, covered, until the bulgur is tender and most of the water has been absorbed, about 15 minutes. Drain and transfer to a medium bowl to cool.

2. When the bulgur is cool, stir in the scallions, cucumber, radishes, carrot, parsley, and mint. Add the tuna with its oil, the olive oil, lemon juice, salt, and pepper. Mix gently to combine.

TABBOULEH TIPS

■ To cook the bulgur traditionally, put it in a bowl, pour boiling water over it, let it soak for about thirty minutes, and drain. The texture will be a bit firmer.

■ The longer tabbouleh sits, the better it gets. As the juices from the vegetables soak into the bulgur, the flavors marry. Try some the next day.

■ Be sure to use the oil from the tuna. If you don't, you'll need to add another tablespoon and a half of olive oil.

OAT CAKES AND SPINACH WITH HORSERADISH SAUCE

Banish all thoughts of gluey morning oatmeal. These crisp oat cakes may change the way you think about the grain. The batter is sticky; so it's easiest to form the cakes right in the pan rather than by hand.

WINE RECOMMENDATION
Many consider Tocai Friulano to be Italy's best white wine. Uncommonly rich, with bracing acidity, Tocai will more than stand up to the spinach and horseradish here.

SERVES 4

2 cups milk
1¾ cups old-fashioned oats
5 tablespoons sour cream
2 teaspoons drained prepared horseradish
1¾ teaspoons salt
2 tablespoons butter
4 tablespoons cooking oil, more if needed
1 onion, chopped
1 carrot, chopped
2 tablespoons cashews, chopped
1 cup chopped fresh parsley
2 eggs, beaten to mix
1 teaspoon fresh-ground black pepper
2 10-ounce packages frozen whole-leaf spinach, defrosted

1. In a medium saucepan, bring the milk to a boil. Stir in the oats and remove from the heat. In a small bowl, combine the sour cream, horseradish, and ¼ teaspoon of the salt.

2. In a large nonstick frying pan, melt 1 tablespoon of the butter with 1 tablespoon of the oil over moderate heat. Add the onion and cook, stirring occasionally, until translucent, about 5 minutes. Add the carrot and cashews and cook, stirring occasionally, until the carrot is tender, about 5 minutes longer. Remove from the heat and stir in the oats.

3. In a bowl, mix the parsley, eggs, 1 teaspoon of salt, ½ teaspoon of pepper, and the oat mixture. Heat 1 tablespoon of the oil in the frying pan over moderate heat. Using a ¼-cup measure, scoop mounds of the oat mixture into the pan and flatten with a spatula. Fry in batches, adding the remaining oil as needed, until golden, about 3 minutes per side. Keep warm in a 200° oven on a baking sheet lined with paper towels.

4. Meanwhile, in a medium saucepan, melt the remaining tablespoon of butter over moderately low heat. Add the spinach and the remaining ½ teaspoon each of salt and pepper. Cover and cook until hot, about 5 minutes. Serve with the oat cakes with the sauce on the side.

Eggs
&
Cheese

ASPARAGUS AND BOK-CHOY FRITTATA

When making an Italian frittata, don't limit yourself to traditional ingredients. The Asian flavors that fill this version offer a real change of pace. Cook the eggs on top of the stove or in the oven—but be sure to use moderate heat so they don't turn rubbery.

 WINE RECOMMENDATION
South Africa is one of the so-called New World wine countries, along with Australia, New Zealand, and the Americas, but its wines best reflect the balance of the European tradition. A South African chardonnay will make a marvelous partner for this Italian-inspired dish.

SERVES 4

2   tablespoons cooking oil

3   scallions including green tops, sliced thin

1   teaspoon grated fresh ginger

1   clove garlic, minced

1   small head bok choy (about ¾ pound), cut into 1-inch pieces

¾   pound asparagus, tough ends snapped off and discarded, spears cut into 1-inch pieces

¾   teaspoon salt

9   eggs, beaten to mix

¼   teaspoon fresh-ground black pepper

1   teaspoon Asian sesame oil

1. Heat the oven to 325°. In a medium cast-iron or ovenproof nonstick frying pan, heat the cooking oil over moderate heat. Add the scallions, ginger, and garlic and cook, stirring, until fragrant, about 30 seconds. Add the bok choy and cook, stirring, until the leaves wilt, about 2 minutes. Add the asparagus and ½ teaspoon of the salt and continue to cook, stirring occasionally, until the vegetables are almost tender, about 3 minutes more.

2. Evenly distribute the vegetables in the pan and then add the eggs, pepper, and the remaining ¼ teaspoon of salt. Cook the frittata, without stirring, until the edges start to set, about 2 minutes. Put the frittata in the oven and bake until firm, about 25 minutes. Drizzle the sesame oil over the top.

THE TRUTH ABOUT EGGS

If you've been avoiding eggs for fear of their high cholesterol content, there's good news: The latest scientific research shows overwhelming evidence that saturated fat, not dietary cholesterol, is what can affect blood cholesterol. Eggs are nutrient dense. In fact, they're the highest-quality source of protein available (after mother's milk) and they're even low in calories (seventy-five per large egg). So for almost everyone, eating an egg or two every day is perfectly fine.

Broccoli-Rabe and Ricotta Frittata

Though frittatas are often served cooled as a first course, they make an equally good main dish, either warm or at room temperature. Here ricotta mellows the bite of broccoli rabe.

WINE RECOMMENDATION

Prosecco, a sparkling wine from Italy's Lombardy region, makes an unexpected accompaniment to this frittata. The wine has a crisp and almost neutral taste, making it very versatile with food. Drink it from a tumbler, as the Italians do.

SERVES 4

¾ pound broccoli rabe, tough stems removed

9 eggs

¾ cup ricotta (about ⅓ pound)

¾ teaspoon salt

½ teaspoon fresh-ground black pepper

2 tablespoons olive oil

1 clove garlic, minced

2 tablespoons grated Parmesan

1. Heat the oven to 325°. In a large pot of boiling, salted water, cook the broccoli rabe until almost tender, about 3 minutes. Drain. Rinse the broccoli rabe with cold water and drain thoroughly. Cut the broccoli rabe into 2-inch lengths and set aside.

2. In a large bowl, beat the eggs with the ricotta and ¼ teaspoon each of the salt and the pepper.

3. In a medium cast-iron or ovenproof nonstick frying pan, heat the oil over moderate heat. Add the garlic and cook, stirring, until fragrant, about 30 seconds. Add the blanched broccoli rabe and the remaining ½ teaspoon salt and ¼ teaspoon pepper and cook, stirring, for 2 minutes.

4. Evenly distribute the broccoli rabe in the pan and then add the egg mixture. Cook the frittata, without stirring, until the edges start to set, about 2 minutes. Sprinkle the Parmesan over the top and bake until firm, about 25 minutes.

Vegetable Tip

Broccoli rabe is, frankly, bitter—usually appealingly so, but sometimes the bitterness can be overwhelming. Blanching the vegetable in boiling salted water for a few minutes before proceeding with the recipe tempers its strength. The trick, used here, can be applied to almost any dish.

BAKED EGGS WITH SPINACH, ASPARAGUS, AND PROSCIUTTO

Bake the eggs, in their nests of crusty bread, until the whites are just set. When you cut into the egg, the still-liquid yolk acts as a sauce. If spicy food is your fancy, try serving a favorite salsa on the side.

WINE RECOMMENDATION
New Zealand sauvignon blancs have a distinctive style, with a powerful streak of acidity, ripe citrus and gooseberry flavors, and a singular note of asparagus. Try one with this egg dish for an intriguing pas de deux.

SERVES 4

- 1 small round loaf crusty bread (about 10 ounces), 2 ends removed, the rest cut into 4 thick slices
- ¾ pound asparagus, tough ends snapped off and discarded, spears cut into 2-inch pieces
- ¼ pound thin-sliced prosciutto
- ¼ pound Gruyère, grated
- 1 10-ounce package frozen chopped spinach, defrosted, drained, and squeezed dry
- 4 eggs
- ¼ teaspoon salt
- ⅛ teaspoon fresh-ground black pepper

1. Heat the oven to 450°. Put the bread on a baking sheet and toast in the oven, turning once, until lightly browned, about 5 minutes in all. Transfer to an oiled baking dish.

2. Meanwhile, bring a medium pot of salted water to a boil. Add the asparagus and cook until tender, about 5 minutes. Drain, rinse with cold water, and drain thoroughly.

3. Using your fingers, make a depression in the center of each slice of bread. Arrange one or two slices of prosciutto around the edge of each slice of bread. Reserve 2 tablespoons of the cheese. Press a quarter of the remaining cheese into the center of each slice of bread. Top the cheese with the spinach, and then surround that with the asparagus. Break an egg into a small dish. Carefully slip the egg into one of the spinach nests. Repeat with remaining eggs. Sprinkle the eggs with the salt and pepper and the reserved cheese. Bake, covered, until the egg whites are just set, 10 to 15 minutes.

CORN PUDDING

Like a soufflé but less temperamental, this pudding can be served either straight from the oven or at room temperature. Don't worry if you can't find fresh corn; frozen kernels work just fine.

WINE RECOMMENDATION
Look for a gentle and fruity merlot from Chile. These wines have the wonderful soft texture and ripe-berry flavors one expects from merlot, along with somewhat earthy undertones that will marry nicely with the corn.

SERVES 4

1½ tablespoons butter

1 onion, chopped

1 green bell pepper, chopped

1 red bell pepper, chopped

1 ¼-pound piece smoked ham, such as Black Forest, cut into ½-inch pieces

¾ teaspoon salt

½ teaspoon fresh-ground black pepper

1 cup fresh (from about 2 ears) or frozen corn kernels

1½ cups half-and-half

6 eggs

1½ teaspoons sugar

⅛ teaspoon cayenne

¼ pound Monterey jack, grated (about 1 cup)

1. Heat the oven to 350°. Butter an 8-by-12-inch baking dish or another shallow baking dish of about the same size. In a medium nonstick frying pan, melt the butter over moderately low heat. Add the onion and cook, stirring occasionally, until translucent, about 5 minutes. Add the bell peppers and cook, stirring occasionally, until the peppers are tender, about 5 minutes more. Stir in the ham, salt, and black pepper and cook, stirring, for 1 minute. Set aside to cool.

2. Meanwhile, combine the corn and half-and-half in a blender or food processor and puree until smooth. Add the eggs, sugar, and cayenne. Blend thoroughly.

3. Spoon the bell-pepper mixture into the prepared baking dish and then sprinkle the Monterey jack over the top. Pour the egg mixture over all. Bake until a toothpick inserted in the center of the pudding comes out clean, about 40 minutes.

VARIATIONS

Omit the ham for a **meatless version**, or replace it with crumbled cooked **chorizo** for a spicier pudding.

ARTICHOKE-HEART, SPINACH, AND MOZZARELLA BREAD PUDDING

Using defrosted frozen vegetables can be a huge time-saver, since they're already cooked, but don't be in too much of a rush; you'll need to take the time to drain and dry them, or the extra moisture will make the finished dish soggy.

WINE RECOMMENDATION
Chardonnays from northern Italy tend to be lighter and crisper than those from California or France. For a delicious partner to this rich bread pudding, see if you can find an unoaked example from the Alto Adige or Trentino.

SERVES 4

2 10-ounce packages frozen chopped spinach, defrosted, drained, and squeezed dry

1 9-ounce package defrosted frozen artichoke hearts, diced and drained on paper towels

3 scallions including green tops, chopped

1 quart ½-inch cubes of good-quality white bread

½ pound grated mozzarella (about 2 cups)

4 eggs

2 cups milk

½ cup grated Parmesan

¾ teaspoon salt

¼ teaspoon fresh-ground black pepper

1. Heat the oven to 350°. Butter an 8-by-12-inch baking dish or a 1½-quart gratin dish. In a large bowl, combine the spinach, artichoke hearts, scallions, bread cubes, and half the mozzarella. Spread this mixture in the bottom of the prepared baking dish. Top with the remaining mozzarella.

2. In a medium bowl, whisk together the eggs, milk, Parmesan, salt, and pepper. Pour over the vegetables and bread and press the bread into the liquid, making sure that it's well moistened.

3. Bake the bread pudding for 20 minutes. Raise the oven temperature to 400° and bake until the pudding is puffed and browned, 15 to 20 minutes longer.

TEST-KITCHEN TIP

Defrost **frozen vegetables** quickly by removing them from the package and putting them into a bowl of hot water. You may need to squeeze or blot the vegetables dry on paper towels before using them, but the defrosting will take only minutes.

BRIE RACLETTE

Swiss raclette, the dish of gently melted cheese (also named *raclette*) that is served with boiled potatoes, air-dried beef, and cornichons, inspired this more accessible version that uses easy-to-find, quick-to-melt Brie.

WINE RECOMMENDATION
The wines of the Loire Valley in France are frequently overlooked by serious imbibers, but its elegant cabernet-franc-based reds are often more suitable at the table than more robust cabernet sauvignons. Go for a fruity Chinon or Saumur-Champigny.

SERVES 4

1½ pounds Brie, rind removed

1½ pounds small new potatoes, or boiling potatoes cut into 1-inch pieces

1½ pounds broccoli, thick stems removed, tops cut into florets (about 1½ quarts)

1½ pounds mushrooms, halved or quartered if large

2 tablespoons cooking oil

½ teaspoon salt

½ cup cocktail onions

1. Heat the oven to 400°. Cut the Brie into thin slices and divide the cheese among four small ovenproof dishes or ramekins.

2. Put the potatoes in a large saucepan of salted water. Bring to a boil and simmer for 10 minutes. Add the broccoli florets to the pan and simmer until the potatoes and broccoli are tender, about 5 minutes longer. Remove the broccoli with a slotted spoon and drain on paper towels. Drain the potatoes and, if using new potatoes, cut them in quarters when cool enough to handle.

3. Meanwhile, toss the mushrooms with the oil and salt. Put the mushrooms on a baking sheet and roast until browned and tender, turning once, 10 to 15 minutes. Remove the pan from the oven and then turn the oven off.

4. Put the dishes of cheese in the oven and leave until the cheese just melts, 5 to 10 minutes. Meanwhile, pile the potatoes, broccoli, mushrooms, and cocktail onions on individual plates. Serve each portion of melted Brie immediately, along with the vegetables for dipping.

VEGETABLE TIP

Cocktail onions, most frequently found in your martini glass, can stand on their own as a pickle. Their slight crunch and pleasant tartness make them surprisingly tasty with Brie.

Zucchini, Corn, Black-Bean, and Jack-Cheese Quesadillas

The grated zucchini and defrosted frozen corn that fill these tasty quesadillas contain a lot of moisture. Drain them on paper towels for a few minutes before using; otherwise, you'd end up with soggy tortillas. Serve the quesadillas with spicy salsa.

WINE RECOMMENDATION

Pull out the stops with a full-throttle red zinfandel from Napa or Amador county. These big, powerful, full-bodied wines are loaded with enough ripe blackberry fruit and exotic spice to match the quesadillas and salsa.

SERVES 4

- 1 small zucchini, grated and drained on paper towels (about 1 cup)
- 1 cup defrosted frozen corn, drained on paper towels
- 1 small red onion, chopped
- 2 jalapeño peppers, seeds and ribs removed, chopped
- 1⅔ cups drained and rinsed canned black beans (one 15-ounce can)
- ½ teaspoon salt
- ¼ teaspoon fresh-ground black pepper
- 1 teaspoon chili powder
- ¾ pound Monterey jack, grated (about 1 quart)
- 8 large (burrito-size) flour tortillas
- 2 tablespoons cooking oil

1. In a large bowl, combine the zucchini, corn, onion, jalapeños, beans, salt, pepper, and chili powder. Toss gently to distribute the seasonings and then stir in the cheese.

2. Heat the oven to 200°. Set the tortillas on a work surface. Put about ⅓ cup of the filling on one half of each tortilla. Spread the filling to the edge and then fold the tortilla over the filling.

3. In a large nonstick frying pan, heat ½ tablespoon of the oil over moderate heat. Add two of the quesadillas to the pan and cook, turning once, until the cheese melts, about 1½ minutes per side. Remove from the pan and keep warm on a baking sheet in the oven. Repeat in batches with the remaining oil and quesadillas. Cut the quesadillas in wedges and serve.

Vegetable Tip

All commercially **frozen vegetables** have already been blanched, so you don't need to cook them for as long as raw vegetables. In fact, some—such as corn, peas, and spinach—don't need to be cooked anymore at all. Just defrost and heat.

EGGPLANT AND GOAT-CHEESE "SANDWICHES" WITH TOMATO TARRAGON SAUCE

Golden eggplant slices sandwich tangy, melting cheese, all set off by a fast tomato sauce flavored with the unusually complementary tarragon.

WINE RECOMMENDATION
Here's a good excuse to sample a northern Italian merlot. Fresh, light-bodied, tart, and aromatic, the wine has plum and herb flavors that will be perfect here. Favor one from Friuli over the richer, often barrel-aged, versions from Tuscany.

SERVES 4

1 tablespoon olive oil

1 small onion, chopped

3 cups canned crushed tomatoes in thick puree (one 28-ounce can)

1½ teaspoons dried tarragon

1¼ teaspoons salt

1 teaspoon sugar

½ teaspoon fresh-ground black pepper

1 cup dry bread crumbs

½ cup grated Parmesan

2 eggplants, peeled and cut to make sixteen ½-inch-thick slices in all

4 eggs, beaten to mix

Cooking oil, for frying

½ pound mild goat cheese, such as Montrachet, cut into 8 rounds

1. In a medium saucepan, heat the olive oil over moderately low heat. Add the onion and cook, stirring occasionally, until translucent, about 5 minutes. Add the tomatoes, tarragon, ¾ teaspoon of the salt, and the sugar and simmer, stirring occasionally, for 25 minutes. Stir in ¼ teaspoon of the pepper.

2. Meanwhile, heat the oven to 350°. In a medium bowl, combine the bread crumbs, Parmesan, and the remaining ½ teaspoon salt and ¼ teaspoon pepper.

3. Dip each slice of eggplant in the eggs and then in the bread-crumb mixture, coating well. In a large frying pan, heat about half an inch of cooking oil over moderate heat until very hot. Fry the eggplant in the hot oil, in batches, turning once, until golden and cooked through, 1 to 2 minutes per side. Drain on paper towels.

4. Arrange half of the eggplant slices in a single layer on a baking sheet. Put a slice of goat cheese on top of each and then top with the remaining eggplant slices. Bake until the cheese melts, about 10 minutes. Put the sauce on plates and top with the eggplant.

Soups

Sweet-and-Sour Cabbage Soup

There's nothing more comforting than a warming bowl of cabbage soup. Ours conjures up memories of beloved, slow-cooked Eastern European versions; yet it's quick to make.

WINE RECOMMENDATION

When it comes to wine, no one does sweet-and-sour like the Germans. It's that dynamic balance between sugar and fruity acidity that makes their wines not only delicious, but a perfect match for this soup. A Pfalz riesling spätlese will have just the right weight and richness.

SERVES 4

¼ pound sliced bacon, cut crosswise into thin strips

1 onion, chopped

2 carrots chopped

3 ribs celery, chopped

1 turnip, peeled and cut into ½-inch dice

1½ teaspoons caraway seeds

1½ pounds green cabbage (about ½ head), shredded (1½ quarts)

7 cups canned low-sodium chicken broth or homemade stock

1⅔ cups canned diced tomatoes with their juice (one 15-ounce can)

1½ tablespoons brown sugar

1½ teaspoons salt

½ teaspoon fresh-ground black pepper

¼ cup cider vinegar

½ cup raisins

¼ cup chopped fresh dill (optional)

Sour cream, for serving (optional)

1. In a large saucepan, cook the bacon over moderate heat until crisp. Remove the bacon with a slotted spoon and drain on paper towels. Pour off all but 1 tablespoon of the fat. Reduce the heat to moderately low. Add the onion, carrots, celery, and turnip and cook, stirring occasionally, until the vegetables start to soften, about 5 minutes.

2. Stir in the caraway seeds, cabbage, and chicken broth and bring to a simmer. Reduce the heat and simmer, covered, until the cabbage wilts, about 5 minutes. Stir in the tomatoes, brown sugar, salt, pepper, vinegar, and raisins. Cover and simmer for 30 minutes.

3. Stir the bacon and the dill, if using, into the soup. Serve the soup topped with a dollop of sour cream, if using.

ASIAN VEGETABLE SOUP WITH NOODLES

The noodles here aren't cooked in the soup; they'd absorb too much of the liquid. Instead, they're boiled separately, tossed with sesame oil, and then put into bowls, waiting to be warmed by the hot broth. The bok choy goes into the soup toward the end of cooking, so that a hint of crispness remains.

 WINE RECOMMENDATION
German wines are huge sellers in Japan; their exciting juxtaposition of tangy acidity, vibrant aromatic fruitiness, and balancing sweetness is ideal for Asian cuisine. Look for a Mosel kabinett for a match made in heaven.

SERVES 4

1 tablespoon cooking oil

6 scallions including green tops, chopped

4 cloves garlic, minced

2 teaspoons chopped fresh ginger

¼ cup soy sauce

¼ teaspoon dried red-pepper flakes

3½ cups water

3½ cups canned low-sodium chicken broth or homemade stock

4 carrots, cut diagonally into ¼-inch slices

¾ pound napa (Chinese) cabbage (about ½ head), leaves shredded (about 3 cups)

¾ teaspoon salt

1 small head bok choy (about ¾ pound), stalks halved lengthwise and cut crosswise into ½-inch pieces, leaves shredded

Grated zest of 1 lemon

2 tablespoons lemon juice

¼ pound vermicelli

1½ teaspoons Asian sesame oil

1. In a large saucepan, heat the cooking oil over moderately low heat. Add the scallions, garlic, and ginger and cook, stirring occasionally, until fragrant, about 1 minute. Add the soy sauce, red-pepper flakes, water, and broth and bring to a boil.

2. Add the carrots to the broth and simmer for 5 minutes. Stir in the cabbage and salt and simmer for 5 minutes longer. Add the bok choy and lemon zest and simmer until the bok choy starts to soften, about 5 minutes. Stir in the lemon juice.

3. Meanwhile, in a large pot of boiling salted water, cook the vermicelli until just done, about 9 minutes. Drain. Return the noodles to the pot and toss with the sesame oil. Put some noodles in each of four bowls and ladle the soup over the noodles.

VEGETABLE NOODLE SOUP

Nothing fancy, nothing new, just a beautifully basic vegetable soup that can accommodate whatever vegetables you have on hand. We've listed plenty of possibilities below, but the variations are infinite.

WINE RECOMMENDATION
With this soup, try one of the lean and aromatic cabernet francs from the North Fork of Long Island, New York. These wines have less tannin than cabernet sauvignon and a distinct herbal, sometimes vegetal, flavor.

SERVES 4

- 2 tablespoons cooking oil
- 2 onions, chopped
- 3 carrots, halved lengthwise and cut crosswise into ½-inch slices
- 2 ribs celery, cut into ½-inch slices
- 1½ quarts canned low-sodium chicken broth or homemade stock
- 1¾ cups canned diced tomatoes with their juice (one 15-ounce can)
- 1 tablespoon tomato paste
- ½ pound potatoes, peeled and cut into ½-inch dice
- ½ pound green beans, halved
- 1¼ teaspoons salt
- 3 ounces fine egg noodles (about 1 cup)
- ⅓ cup chopped fresh parsley

1. In a large saucepan, heat the oil over moderately low heat. Add the onions, carrots, and celery and cook, stirring occasionally, until the vegetables start to soften, about 10 minutes. Stir in the broth, tomatoes, tomato paste, potatoes, green beans, and salt. Bring to a boil. Reduce the heat and simmer, partially covered, until the vegetables are almost tender, about 20 minutes.

2. Stir in the egg noodles. Bring the soup back to a simmer and cook until the vegetables and noodles are tender, about 5 minutes. Stir in the parsley.

VARIATIONS

Feel free to mix and match **vegetable combinations** according to what you like and what you have on hand. Other excellent soup vegetables include: fennel, celery root, cabbage, parsnips, turnips, peas, zucchini, squash, shredded greens, corn, lima beans, and bell peppers.

CORN CHOWDER

Our simple soup really highlights the taste of sweet summer corn, but since the vegetable is available virtually all the time, you can make the chowder year-round. You can even use frozen corn, though fresh is best.

WINE RECOMMENDATION
Chardonnay seems to have an affinity for corn; perhaps it is the sweet buttery flavors that complement each other so well. For best effect with this chowder, pick a rich, full-bodied example from southeastern Australia.

SERVES 4

2 tablespoons butter

4 scallions, white bulbs and green tops chopped and reserved separately

1 red bell pepper, chopped

2 ribs celery, chopped

1 pound boiling potatoes (about 3), peeled and cut into $\frac{1}{2}$-inch dice

4 cups fresh corn kernels (cut from about 8 ears)

1 bay leaf

1 quart canned low-sodium chicken broth or homemade stock

2 teaspoons salt

2 cups milk

$\frac{1}{4}$ teaspoon fresh-ground black pepper

Sour cream, for serving (optional)

1. In a large saucepan, melt the butter over moderately low heat. Add the scallion bulbs, bell pepper, and celery and cook, stirring occasionally, until the vegetables start to soften, about 10 minutes. Stir in the potatoes, 2 cups of the corn, the bay leaf, broth, and salt. Bring to a boil. Reduce the heat and simmer, stirring occasionally, for 15 minutes.

2. In a blender or food processor, puree the remaining 2 cups corn with the milk. Stir the puree into the soup along with the black pepper. Simmer until the soup thickens slightly, 5 to 10 minutes. Remove the bay leaf. Stir in the scallion greens. Top each serving with a dollop of sour cream, if using.

FROZEN-CORN VARIATION

If you want to use frozen corn, puree two cups of it with the milk as directed above, and add the remaining two cups to the soup along with the puree. Since the corn is already cooked, it might toughen if it goes in earlier. You could add a pinch of sugar, too.

GREEN MINESTRONE

Swiss chard, spinach, celery—this soup is a veritable sea of greens. Potatoes, pasta, and Parmesan give it substance and, along with the fennel, a distinctly Italian feel.

WINE RECOMMENDATION
Your best bet with all these greens is a charming, fruity red, such as a Beaujolais or Valpolicella. The bright berry flavors will contrast with and highlight the vegetables.

SERVES 4

- 3 tablespoons olive oil
- 1 onion, chopped
- 1 fennel bulb, chopped
- 3 ribs celery, chopped
- 1½ teaspoons salt
- 1 pound boiling potatoes (about 3), peeled and cut into ½-inch cubes
- 1 quart canned low-sodium chicken broth or homemade stock
- 3 cups water
- ¼ teaspoon fresh-ground black pepper
- ½ cup tubetti or other small macaroni
- ½ pound Swiss chard, tough stems removed, leaves washed well and shredded (about 3 cups)
- 1 pound spinach, stems removed, leaves washed well and shredded (about 5 cups)
- ⅓ cup grated Parmesan

1. In a large saucepan, heat the oil over moderately low heat. Add the onion, fennel, celery, and ¼ teaspoon of the salt. Cook, stirring occasionally, until the vegetables start to soften, about 10 minutes.

2. Add the potatoes, broth, water, the remaining 1¼ teaspoons salt, and the pepper. Bring to a boil. Reduce the heat and simmer for 5 minutes. Stir in the pasta and simmer for 5 minutes longer.

3. Add the Swiss chard and spinach and bring the soup back to a simmer. Cook, stirring occasionally, until the greens are wilted and the pasta is tender, about 5 minutes longer. Stir in the Parmesan.

VARIATIONS

You'll need a total of eight cups of shredded greens for this soup. Use one or any combination of the following: **Swiss chard, spinach, escarole, green cabbage,** or **kale.** The more variety the better.

ISLAND KALE AND SWEET-POTATO SOUP

Inspired by Caribbean callaloo, this tropical, coconut-milk-spiked soup can be mildly or wildly spicy, according to your taste. If you like it hot, add some or all of the jalapeño seeds or a splash of Tabasco sauce.

WINE RECOMMENDATION

Foods with a bit of sweetness invite some in the wine as well. Good choices would include an off-dry chenin blanc from California or a similarly off-dry riesling from Washington State.

SERVES 4

- 2 tablespoons cooking oil
- 1 onion, chopped
- 2 cloves garlic, minced
- 1 jalapeño pepper, seeds and ribs removed, sliced thin
- ¾ pound kale, tough stems removed, leaves washed well and shredded (about 1 quart)
- 1½ pounds sweet potatoes (about 3), peeled and cut into ¾-inch cubes
- 1½ quarts canned low-sodium chicken broth or homemade stock
- 1½ teaspoons salt
- 1 cup canned unsweetened coconut milk
- 1 cup long-grain rice

1. In a large saucepan, heat the oil over moderately low heat. Add the onion and cook, stirring occasionally, until translucent, about 5 minutes. Stir in the garlic and jalapeño and cook, stirring, until fragrant, about 30 seconds.

2. Stir in the kale, sweet potatoes, broth, and salt and bring to a boil. Reduce the heat and simmer, partially covered, until the potatoes are tender, about 20 minutes. Add the coconut milk and just heat through.

3. Meanwhile, bring a medium pot of salted water to a boil. Stir in the rice and boil until just done, 10 to 12 minutes. Drain. Put a mound of rice in the center of each bowl. Ladle the soup around the rice.

VEGETABLE TIP

Crinkly **kale** leaves are wonderfully sturdy and flavorful, making them especially well-suited to soups. Remove and discard the thick stems and then wash the leaves really well before adding them to a dish. The twists and turns of kale leaves are great places for dirt to hide.

POTATO AND CHEDDAR-CHEESE SOUP

A few simple ingredients make a sumptuous soup. Be sure to use a high-quality cheddar; it's crucial to the dish's flavor. Choose a yellow cheese for the richest color. For a chunkier soup, skip the pureeing and just break up some of the potato with a spoon.

 WINE RECOMMENDATION
Serve a Washington State merlot with this rich and smoky soup. Merlots from Washington's Columbia and Yakima Valleys are a bit more restrained than their brethren from California and have a distinct mineral undercurrent that makes them a natural here.

SERVES 4

¼ pound sliced bacon, cut crosswise into thin strips

1 large onion, chopped

3 pounds baking potatoes (about 6), peeled and cut into 1-inch cubes

4½ cups water

1 teaspoon salt

6 ounces cheddar, grated (about 1½ cups)

¼ cup chopped chives or scallion tops

1. In a large saucepan, cook the bacon over moderate heat until crisp. Remove the bacon with a slotted spoon and drain on paper towels. Pour off all but 2 tablespoons of the bacon fat or, if you don't have 2 tablespoons, add enough cooking oil to make up the amount. Reduce the heat to moderately low.

2. Add the onion and cook, stirring occasionally, until translucent, about 5 minutes. Stir in the potatoes, water, and salt and bring to a boil. Reduce the heat and simmer, covered, stirring occasionally, until the potatoes are tender, 15 to 20 minutes.

3. Remove half the soup from the pan and puree in a food processor. Alternatively, mash some of the potatoes with a potato masher. Return the puree to the pan. Over low heat, add the cheese and stir until melted. Remove the pan from the heat. Taste the soup and add more salt if needed. Serve the soup topped with the bacon and chives.

VEGETABLE TIP

Boiling **potatoes** have less starch than baking, or Idaho, potatoes and consequentially hold together better when boiled. This is why they're often used in soups and for potato salads. Not in this soup, though. Since we *want* some of the potato to break down into smaller pieces and thicken the soup, baking potatoes are the perfect choice.

CARROT, SQUASH, AND JERUSALEM-ARTICHOKE SOUP WITH WHITE BEANS

Colorful vegetables brighten our satisfying, brothy soup. If Jerusalem artichokes (also called sunchokes) aren't available in your area, substitute another flavorful, slightly starchy vegetable such as parsnips or turnips, or simply increase the quantities of the other vegetables in the soup.

WINE RECOMMENDATION
The soft nutty flavors and rich texture of pinot gris beautifully complement the earthy sweetness of this tasty soup. Try one from a well-known Alsace producer such as Trimbach, Sparr, Beyer, or Hugel.

SERVES 4

2 tablespoons olive oil

1 onion, chopped

1 pound carrots, halved lengthwise and cut crosswise into ½-inch slices

1¾ teaspoons salt

2 cloves garlic, minced

1 zucchini, quartered lengthwise and cut crosswise into ½-inch slices

1 yellow squash, quartered lengthwise and cut crosswise into ½-inch slices

1½ quarts canned low-sodium chicken broth or homemade stock

1⅔ cups canned diced tomatoes with their juice (one 15-ounce can)

1 pound Jerusalem artichokes, peeled, halved, and cut into ½-inch slices

3 cups drained and rinsed canned cannellini beans (two 15-ounce cans)

½ cup chopped fresh parsley

¼ teaspoon fresh-ground black pepper

Grated zest of ½ orange

1. In a large saucepan, heat the oil over moderate heat. Add the onion, carrots, and ½ teaspoon of the salt and cook, stirring occasionally, until the vegetables start to soften, about 5 minutes.

2. Add the garlic, zucchini, yellow squash, broth, tomatoes, and the remaining 1¼ teaspoons salt; bring to a simmer. Add the Jerusalem artichokes and return to a simmer. Reduce the heat and simmer, partially covered, until the vegetables are tender, about 10 minutes. Stir in the beans, parsley, pepper, and zest.

VEGETABLE TIP

If you don't want to tackle the job of peeling knobby **Jerusalem artichokes**, just scrub them well with a vegetable brush under running water and leave the peel on.

BLACK-BEAN SOUP WITH AVOCADO SALSA

Black beans, often served in a soup or stew, have been a mainstay of Mexican cuisine for thousands of years. Black-bean soup is also popular in the Caribbean, where rum, sherry, or peppered wine is often added toward the end of cooking. We add the sherry somewhat earlier in this version, which combines elements of both traditions.

WINE RECOMMENDATION
Don't forget about sherries when considering wines for the table. They work particularly well with soups, especially when sherry is an ingredient already. With this black-bean soup, a dry amontillado is a natural.

SERVES 4

6 cups drained and rinsed canned black beans (three 19-ounce cans)

4 cups canned low-sodium chicken broth or homemade stock

2 tablespoons cooking oil

1 onion, chopped

1½ teaspoons salt

½ cup dry sherry

1 teaspoon fresh-ground black pepper

2 avocados, preferably Hass, cut into ½-inch dice

¼ cup chopped cilantro or flat-leaf parsley

6 radishes, halved and sliced thin

2 tablespoons lime juice

1. Combine 3 cups of the beans and 1 cup of chicken broth in a blender or food processor and puree until smooth.

2. In a large saucepan, heat the oil over moderate heat. Add the onion and 1 teaspoon of the salt and cook, stirring frequently, until the onion is soft, about 5 minutes. Increase the heat, add the sherry, and boil until reduced to approximately ¼ cup, about 3 minutes.

3. Add the bean puree, ½ teaspoon of the pepper, and the remaining 3 cups of chicken broth and 3 cups of beans. Simmer until hot, about 5 minutes.

4. Meanwhile, in a small bowl, combine the avocados, cilantro, radishes, lime juice, and the remaining ½ teaspoon each of salt and pepper. Mix gently. Spoon the soup into bowls and top with the salsa.

VEGETABLE TIP

If the **radishes** aren't perfectly crisp, soak them in a bowl of ice water. A few minutes of shock may be just enough to revive them.

LENTIL SOUP WITH BROCCOLI RABE

Cook the broccoli rabe in a separate pan, not in the soup pot. That way, any excess bitterness from the vegetable goes down the drain with the cooking water rather than into the soup. You'll find, though, that a bit of bite enlivens the lentils.

WINE RECOMMENDATION
This is a great time to turn to an old friend, Beaujolais. The wine's frank fruitiness, soft texture, and lively acidity will contrast with the lentils and will blunt the bitterness of the broccoli rabe.

SERVES 4

- 2 tablespoons cooking oil
- 1 onion, chopped
- 2 carrots, chopped
- 2 ribs celery, chopped
- 1 clove garlic, minced
- 1 pound lentils (2 cups)
- 2½ quarts water
- 2 tablespoons tomato paste
- 1 bay leaf
- 2¼ teaspoons salt
- ¼ teaspoon fresh-ground black pepper
- 1 pound broccoli rabe, cut into 1½-inch lengths (about 2 quarts)
  Grated zest of 1½ lemons

1. In a large saucepan, heat the oil over moderately low heat. Add the onion and cook, stirring occasionally, until translucent, about 5 minutes. Stir in the carrots, celery, and garlic and cook, stirring occasionally, until the vegetables start to soften, about 5 minutes.

2. Stir in the lentils, water, tomato paste, bay leaf, salt, and pepper. Bring to a boil. Reduce the heat and simmer, partially covered, stirring occasionally, until the lentils are tender, about 30 minutes.

3. Meanwhile, in a large pot of boiling, salted water, cook the broccoli rabe until just tender, about 5 minutes. Drain.

4. Stir the lemon zest into the soup. Remove the bay leaf. Ladle the soup into bowls and top each serving with some of the broccoli rabe.

VARIATIONS

- Omit the broccoli rabe. Shred ten ounces of raw **spinach**, **escarole**, or **Swiss chard** leaves and stir them into the soup five minutes before it's done.
- The **lentil soup** is also delicious on its own, without any greens at all.

RIBOLLITA

In Italy, *ribollita* (literally *reboiled*) usually means leftovers. And indeed this Tuscan soup is delicious leftover or cooked in advance and reheated. Our recipe is also fantastic if you polish it off the minute it's done, which happens whenever we make it.

WINE RECOMMENDATION
Tuscan cooking doesn't get any more traditional than this. No wonder this soup's perfect partner is Chianti Classico from Tuscany's cultural, spiritual, and gastronomic heartland.

SERVES 4

2 cups drained and rinsed canned cannellini beans (one 19-ounce can)

4 cups water, more if needed

3 slices bacon, cut crosswise into 1/4-inch strips

3/4 teaspoon dried rosemary, crumbled

1 onion, chopped

2 cloves garlic, minced

2 carrots, chopped

1 rib celery, chopped

3/4 pound cabbage (about 1/2 small head), chopped (about 3 cups)

3/4 pound Swiss chard, tough stems removed, leaves washed well and chopped

2 teaspoons salt

1 teaspoon fresh-ground black pepper

2 cups canned tomatoes with their juice (from a 28-ounce can)

2 1 1/4-inch-thick slices country bread

1. Heat the oven to 350°. In a food processor, combine 1 cup of the beans with 1 cup of the water and puree until smooth. Set aside.

2. In a large saucepan, cook the bacon over moderate heat, stirring frequently, for 3 minutes. Add the rosemary, onion, garlic, carrots, and celery and cook, stirring frequently, until the vegetables start to soften, about 10 minutes. Add the cabbage, chard, salt, and pepper and cook, stirring, until the cabbage wilts, about 3 minutes. Stir in the tomatoes and cook, breaking them up with the back of a spoon, for 1 to 2 minutes. Add the remaining 3 cups of water and bring to a simmer. Stir in the bean puree and simmer for 15 minutes.

3. Meanwhile, put the bread on a baking sheet and toast until golden, turning once, about 15 minutes. Add the remaining beans and the toasted bread to the soup. Increase the heat to moderately high and bring just to a boil, stirring to break up the bread. If the soup is too thick, stir in some additional water.

Salads

CAESAR SALAD WITH SHIITAKE MUSHROOMS

Order a Caesar salad at a restaurant these days, and it's likely to be a whole meal, topped with chicken or shrimp. We choose meaty shiitake mushrooms here and also make another break from tradition: The eggs in the dressing are cooked, not raw.

 WINE RECOMMENDATION
Because sparkling wines have surprisingly high acidity, a nonvintage brut Champagne will go well with this salad, matching the vinegar in the dressing and cutting the Parmesan's richness.

SERVES 4

8	tablespoons olive oil
½	pound sourdough baguette, cut into 1-inch cubes (about 1 quart)
¾	teaspoon salt
¾	teaspoon fresh-ground black pepper
4	cloves garlic, minced
1	tablespoon cooking oil
¾	pound shiitake mushrooms, stems removed, caps sliced
½	cup chopped fresh parsley
2	hard-cooked eggs
3	tablespoons wine vinegar
2½	teaspoons anchovy paste
2	small heads romaine lettuce (about 1 pound each), cut crosswise into ½-inch strips (about 5 quarts)
¼	cup grated Parmesan

1. In a large nonstick frying pan, heat 3 tablespoons of the olive oil over moderate heat. Add the cubed bread, ½ teaspoon salt, and ¼ teaspoon pepper and stir to coat the bread with the oil. Sauté the bread until crisp and lightly browned, about 5 minutes. Remove from the heat and stir in half the garlic. Transfer to a large salad bowl.

2. In the same pan, heat the cooking oil over moderately high heat. Add the mushrooms, ¼ teaspoon pepper, and the remaining ¼ teaspoon salt. Cook, stirring frequently, until the mushrooms are tender, 2 to 3 minutes. Add half the remaining garlic and the parsley and cook, stirring, for 1 minute longer. Add the mushrooms to the croutons.

3. Put the eggs, vinegar, anchovy paste, and the remaining garlic, ¼ teaspoon pepper, and 5 tablespoons olive oil in a blender or food processor and whir until smooth. Add the lettuce to the mushrooms and croutons, sprinkle with Parmesan, and then add the dressing. Toss to coat.

FAVORITE-FLAVORS SALAD

We set out to make a cobb salad but got distracted by some of our favorite nibbles—slices of pear, toasted walnuts, pickled onions. The result is a salad that's so much fun you barely notice it's a well-balanced meal. For a dramatic presentation, arrange the ingredients in strips over the lettuce, cobb-salad style, then toss the salad at the table.

WINE RECOMMENDATION
There's only one grape we can think of that can handle blue cheese, walnuts, avocado, *and* vinegar. Riesling it is, and an off-dry kabinett from Germany's Mosel is the one you want.

SERVES 4

1 cup walnut pieces

1 baking potato (about ½ pound), peeled and cut into ¾-inch pieces

½ pound Roquefort or other blue cheese, crumbled

¼ cup wine vinegar

¾ teaspoon salt

¼ teaspoon fresh-ground black pepper

½ cup mild oil, such as canola

1 head romaine lettuce (about 1¼ pounds), cut crosswise into ½-inch strips (about 3 quarts)

2 bunches watercress (about 10 ounces in all), tough stems removed, leaves chopped (about 1 quart)

1 cup drained cocktail onions

1 avocado, preferably Hass, cut into ½-inch dice

1 pear, peeled, cored, and sliced

1. In a small frying pan, toast the nuts over moderately low heat, stirring frequently, until golden brown, about 5 minutes. Or toast them in a 350° oven for 5 to 10 minutes.

2. Put the potato in a medium pot of salted water. Bring to a boil and simmer until tender, about 10 minutes. Drain and set aside.

3. Meanwhile, in a large glass or stainless-steel bowl, combine one third of the blue cheese with the vinegar, salt, and pepper. Mix thoroughly and then gradually whisk in the oil. Reserve 2 tablespoons of the dressing. Add the romaine to the rest of the dressing and toss. Transfer to a platter or salad bowl.

4. Toss the watercress with the reserved dressing. Arrange the remaining blue cheese, the watercress, walnuts, potato, onions, avocado, and pear slices on top of the lettuce.

SPINACH, WHITE-BEAN, AND RED-ONION SALAD

A spinach salad with bonus bacon flavor: The bacon is cooked until crisp and removed, and then the onions and beans are cooked in the drippings. Some of this luscious mixture is tossed with the lettuce and the rest is piled on toasty croûtes to go with the salad.

WINE RECOMMENDATION

The complex combination of flavors and textures in this salad is best accompanied by a simple, crisp, and fruity red wine for contrast. Beaujolais would be our first choice, but Valpolicella, Bardolino, or even a Provençal rosé will work as well.

SERVES 4

4   ¾-inch-thick slices country bread or sourdough bread

¼   pound sliced bacon, cut crosswise into ½-inch strips

2   red onions, sliced thin

3   tablespoons wine vinegar

4   cups drained and rinsed canned cannellini beans (two 19-ounce cans)

1¼ teaspoons salt

1   teaspoon fresh-ground black pepper

4   pounds spinach, stems removed, leaves washed well

2   tablespoons olive oil

1. Heat the oven to 450°. Put the bread on a baking sheet and toast until lightly browned, turning once, about 5 minutes.

2. In a large frying pan, cook the bacon over moderate heat until crisp. Remove the bacon with a slotted spoon and drain on paper towels.

3. Add the onions to the bacon fat and cook over moderate heat, stirring occasionally, until translucent, about 5 minutes. Add 2 tablespoons of the vinegar, the beans, ¾ teaspoon of the salt, and ½ teaspoon of the pepper. Mix gently and remove from the heat.

4. Put the spinach in a large glass or stainless-steel bowl. Add the remaining tablespoon of vinegar and ½ teaspoon each of salt and pepper, the oil, and the bacon to the bowl and toss. Stir half of the bean mixture into the spinach and put the salad on plates. Top each slice of toasted bread with the remaining bean mixture and serve with the salad.

Warm Portobello-Mushroom and Potato Salad

The salad is wonderful either warm or at room temperature, but the meaty mushrooms are juiciest straight from the broiler. They're great cooked on the grill, too, or in a grill pan. If you want to experiment with different greens, try arugula or Belgian endive.

WINE RECOMMENDATION
Wines made from the sémillon grape are rich, full-bodied, and intense, and yet they are surprisingly compatible with a number of cuisines. Look for one from the Hunter Valley of Australia for an interesting and tasty accompaniment for this salad.

SERVES 4

- 4 portobello mushrooms (about 1½ pounds), stems removed, dark underside of caps scraped off
- ⅓ cup plus 6 tablespoons olive oil
- 1¼ teaspoons dried thyme
- 1 teaspoon salt
- ½ teaspoon fresh-ground black pepper
- 1 pound boiling potatoes (about 3), peeled and cut into ¾-inch dice
- 2 teaspoons Dijon mustard
- 1½ tablespoons wine vinegar
- 4 scallions including green tops, chopped
- 1 bunch watercress (about 5 ounces), tough stems removed (about 3 cups)
- 1 small head curly endive (about ¾ pound), torn into bite-size pieces (about 2½ quarts)

1. Heat the broiler. Put the mushroom caps on a baking sheet. In a small bowl, combine the ⅓ cup oil, 1 teaspoon of the thyme, ½ teaspoon salt, and ¼ teaspoon pepper. Pour the mixture over the mushrooms and toss to coat. Broil the mushrooms, turning once, until tender and golden, 6 to 8 minutes per side.

2. Meanwhile, put the potatoes in a medium saucepan of salted water. Bring to a boil and simmer until tender, 5 to 10 minutes. Drain.

3. In a small glass or stainless-steel bowl, mix together the mustard, vinegar, and the remaining ¼ teaspoon thyme, ½ teaspoon salt, and ¼ teaspoon pepper. Add the 6 tablespoons oil slowly, whisking. Toss the warm potatoes with 2 tablespoons of the dressing.

4. In a large bowl, combine the scallions, watercress, and curly endive. Toss with the remaining dressing and then put the greens on a platter or individual plates. Scatter the warm dressed potatoes over the greens. Slice the mushrooms and serve on top of the salad.

CURLY-ENDIVE SALAD
WITH POTATO-AND-APPLE PANCAKES

Hot, crunchy pancakes on top of cool, crisp greens, with a sour-cream dressing thrown in for good measure—this is a heavenly combination. A food processor makes quick work of grating the potatoes, apples, and onion for the pancakes.

WINE RECOMMENDATION
Fuller in body than those from Germany, dry rieslings from Alsace will stand up better to the flavors in this dish.

SERVES 4

- 1/3 cup sour cream
- 1/4 cup milk
- 2 tablespoons chopped fresh chives or scallion tops
- 1/4 teaspoon wine vinegar
- 1¾ teaspoons salt
- 1¼ teaspoons fresh-ground black pepper
- 1 pound baking potatoes (about 2), peeled
- 3 tart apples, such as Granny Smith, cored
- 1 small onion
- 1/4 cup chopped fresh parsley
- 2 eggs, beaten to mix
- 1/2 cup dry bread crumbs
- 2 to 3 tablespoons cooking oil
- 1 small head curly endive (about ¾ pound), torn into bite-size pieces (about 2½ quarts)
- 1 small head red- or green-leaf lettuce (about ½ pound), torn into bite-size pieces (about 1½ quarts)

1. In a small glass or stainless-steel bowl, combine the sour cream, milk, chives, vinegar, ½ teaspoon of the salt, and ¼ teaspoon of the pepper. Mix well and set aside.

2. In a food processor with a grating attachment, grate the potatoes, 1½ of the apples, and the onion. Transfer to a large bowl and stir in the parsley, eggs, bread crumbs, and the remaining 1¼ teaspoons salt and 1 teaspoon pepper.

3. In a large nonstick frying pan, heat 1 tablespoon of the oil over moderate heat. Form the potato mixture into twelve pancakes about 2½ inches wide and ½-inch thick, using about ¼ cup of the mixture for each. Cook the pancakes in batches, turning once, until crisp and golden, 3 to 4 minutes per side. Keep the cooked pancakes warm in a 200° oven on a baking sheet lined with paper towels until the last batch is done. Use 1 tablespoon of oil for each batch.

4. Cut the remaining apples into thin slices. Put them in a large bowl along with the greens. Add all but 2 tablespoons of the dressing and toss. Arrange the salad on plates and top with the pancakes. Drizzle the remaining dressing over the pancakes.

LENTILS VINAIGRETTE

The toasted almonds here lift plain-old lentil salad (plenty good enough on its own) to star status. If you really want to gild the lily, use the small, green lentils du Puy from France. Layering salad on salad—dressed lentils over mixed greens—makes a whole meal.

WINE RECOMMENDATION
The unique earthy flavor of the lentils and the tangy vinaigrette call out for the delicate balance of sweet and tart found in a riesling kabinett from Germany's Mosel region.

SERVES 4

1½   cups lentils

1   quart water

2½   teaspoons salt

7   tablespoons olive or other oil, such as peanut

4   tablespoons wine vinegar

1   red onion, chopped

2   carrots, chopped

2   ribs celery, chopped

¼   teaspoon fresh-ground black pepper

1   cup sliced almonds

½   cup chopped fresh parsley

¼   pound mixed salad greens (about 2 quarts)

1. Put the lentils in a medium saucepan with the water and ½ teaspoon of the salt. Bring to a boil. Reduce the heat to moderate and simmer, partially covered, until the lentils are tender, about 25 minutes. Drain and return to the pan. Add 1 tablespoon of the oil, 1 tablespoon of the vinegar, and ½ teaspoon of the salt. Mix gently and set aside.

2. Meanwhile, in a large nonstick frying pan, heat 3 tablespoons of the oil over moderately low heat. Add the onion and cook, stirring occasionally, until translucent, about 5 minutes. Add the carrots, celery, pepper, and 1 teaspoon of the salt. Cook, stirring occasionally, until the vegetables are tender, about 10 minutes. Remove from the heat and add 2 tablespoons of the vinegar. Combine the cooked lentils with the vegetables.

3. In a small frying pan, toast the almonds over moderately low heat, stirring frequently, until golden brown, 5 to 10 minutes. Or toast them in a 350° oven for 5 to 10 minutes. Shortly before serving, stir the almonds and parsley into the lentil mixture. Put the greens in a large glass or stainless-steel bowl and toss with the remaining 3 tablespoons oil, 1 tablespoon vinegar, and ½ teaspoon salt. Serve the lentil mixture over the greens.

ROASTED VEGETABLES WITH AIOLI

Drizzle vegetables with olive oil, roast them in the oven until tender, and serve—what could be simpler? With a garlicky, lemon-tinged mayonnaise sauce, you have a feast.

WINE RECOMMENDATION
Roasted vegetables and pungent aioli are best partnered with a fairly neutral-flavored, high-acid wine with some body. Italy's Collio region produces delicious pinot grigios that perfectly match that description.

SERVES 4

1 cup mayonnaise

3 cloves garlic, minced

5 tablespoons olive oil

½ teaspoon lemon juice

Pinch cayenne

Salt

1½ pounds baking potatoes (about 3), peeled and cut into approximately 4-by-½-inch sticks

5 carrots, cut into approximately 2½-by-½-inch sticks

2 red bell peppers, cut into ½-inch strips

1 pound asparagus, tough ends snapped off

3 hard-cooked eggs, peeled and quartered

1. Heat the oven to 450°. In a small bowl, combine the mayonnaise, garlic, 2 tablespoons of the oil, the lemon juice, cayenne, and a pinch of salt. Mix well and refrigerate until ready to use.

2. Put the potatoes and carrots on a large baking sheet and toss them with 2 tablespoons of the oil and ½ teaspoon salt. Spread the vegetables out in a single layer and roast them in the oven for 15 minutes.

3. Meanwhile, put the bell-pepper strips on a second large baking sheet and toss them with 1 teaspoon of the oil and ⅛ teaspoon salt. After 15 minutes, take the first pan out of the oven and turn the vegetables with a spatula. Put both pans in the oven and roast for 5 minutes. Toss the asparagus with the remaining 2 teaspoons of oil and ⅛ teaspoon salt. Put the asparagus on the pan with the peppers. Roast until all the vegetables are tender, about 10 minutes longer. Serve the roasted vegetables and hard-cooked eggs with the aioli.

VARIATIONS

Plenty of other vegetables lend themselves to roasting. Try wedges of **sweet potato** or **fennel**, whole **scallions** or **mushrooms**, or halved **Brussels sprouts**.

GADO GADO

Here's a unique, easy-to-assemble Indonesian salad that you can vary every time you make it. We've given our favorite vegetable combination below, but cabbage, bean sprouts, cauliflower, celery, and spinach are also commonly used, and sliced hard-cooked eggs, fried onions or tofu, or sliced tomatoes are popular garnishes. In a true Indonesian meal, rice would be served along with the vegetables and peanut sauce.

WINE RECOMMENDATION

Riesling and Asian food go together like Romeo and Juliet. Did you know that great rieslings are made in Australia's Clare Valley? Some are now being imported into the U.S., and this would be a great time to try one.

SERVES 4

- 2 pounds boiling potatoes (about 6), peeled and cut into 1-inch chunks
- 1 pound green beans
- 8 carrots, cut diagonally into 1-inch chunks
- 1 pound broccoli, thick stems removed, tops cut into small florets (about 1 quart)
- ½ cup peanut butter
- 2 cloves garlic, crushed
- ½ teaspoon red-pepper flakes
- 1 tablespoon brown sugar
- ¼ cup lemon juice (from about 1 lemon)
- 1 tablespoon soy sauce
- ¾ teaspoon salt
- 1 cup hot water
- 2 scallions including green tops, chopped
- ⅓ cup chopped cilantro (optional)
- 2 cucumbers, peeled, halved lengthwise, seeded, and cut into ½-inch strips
- ⅓ cup toasted sunflower seeds or chopped peanuts, for garnish (optional)

1. Bring two medium saucepans of salted water to a boil. Add the potatoes to one of the pans and cook until tender, about 10 minutes. Remove with a slotted spoon and drain well. Meanwhile, cook the green beans in the other pan until tender, about 4 minutes. Remove with a slotted spoon and drain well. As a pan becomes available, cook the carrots and broccoli, separately, until just tender, about 4 minutes each. Drain the vegetables well.

2. Meanwhile, puree the peanut butter, garlic, red-pepper flakes, brown sugar, lemon juice, soy sauce, salt, and hot water in a blender. Put one of the empty saucepans over moderately low heat. Pour the sauce into the pan and warm through. Stir in the scallions and cilantro.

3. Pour a little sauce on one large platter or individual plates. Arrange all the vegetables in small piles over the sauce. Sprinkle with the seeds or nuts and serve with the remaining sauce.

BASMATI-RICE SALAD WITH CAULIFLOWER AND POTATOES

Garlic, fresh ginger, mustard, and a medley of spices spark the hallowed Indian combination—cauliflower, potatoes, and rice. Serve it at room temperature, either alone or with a simple side of sliced tomatoes.

WINE RECOMMENDATION
Basmati's spice and jasmine aromas suggest a floral Vouvray from France's Loire Valley. You'll need a demi-sec to stand up to the spices here.

SERVES 4

1½ cups basmati rice, rinsed

2 tablespoons plain yogurt

3 tablespoons cooking oil

2 onions, sliced thin

2 cloves garlic, minced

1 tablespoon minced fresh ginger

¾ teaspoon dry mustard

¼ teaspoon ground cumin

¼ teaspoon cayenne

¼ teaspoon ground coriander

⅛ teaspoon ground cloves

2 teaspoons salt

1 head cauliflower (about 2 pounds), cut into small florets

1 pound baking potatoes (about 2), peeled and cut into ½-inch dice

3 tablespoons raisins

3 to 4 tablespoons cider or wine vinegar

3½ cups water

½ cup chopped cilantro

4 scallions including green tops, chopped

1. Bring a medium pot of salted water to a boil. Stir in the rice; boil until just done, 10 to 15 minutes. Drain and transfer to a large bowl. Let the rice cool slightly and then stir in the yogurt.

2. Meanwhile, in a large frying pan, heat the oil over moderate heat. Add the onions and cook, stirring occasionally, until translucent, about 5 minutes. Add the garlic, ginger, mustard, cumin, cayenne, coriander, cloves, and 1¾ teaspoons of the salt and cook, stirring, for 1 minute. Stir in the cauliflower, potatoes, and raisins and coat with the spices. Add 2 tablespoons of the vinegar and the water and bring to a boil. Reduce the heat and simmer, covered, until the potatoes are almost tender, about 10 minutes. Uncover, raise the heat, and simmer until almost no liquid remains in the pan, about 10 minutes more.

3. Add the cauliflower mixture to the rice. Stir in the remaining ¼ teaspoon of salt, 1 tablespoon vinegar, the cilantro, and scallions. Taste the salad and, if necessary, add the remaining 1 tablespoon vinegar.

BLACK-BEAN AND YELLOW-RICE SALAD

While perfectly delicious as is, this festive bean-and-rice salad also lends itself to endless variation. Replace the tomatoes with diced avocado; switch the bell pepper from green to red; stir in chopped scallion, red onion, cilantro—whatever suits your taste or whatever you have around.

WINE RECOMMENDATION
An unpretentious, exuberantly fruity, and robust red wine will suit this salad well. Look to Australia for one of its many delicious shiraz that just ooze blackberry and chocolate flavors. They're frequently incredible values, too.

SERVES 4

    3 tablespoons cooking oil
    1 onion, chopped
    2 cloves garlic, minced
  1/4 teaspoon turmeric
  1/2 teaspoon ground cumin
 1 1/4 teaspoons salt
  1/4 teaspoon fresh-ground black pepper
 1 1/2 cups long-grain rice
 2 3/4 cups water
    1 bay leaf
 1 2/3 cups drained and rinsed canned black beans
       (from one 15-ounce can)
    1 green bell pepper, chopped
    2 tomatoes, diced
    1 tablespoon wine vinegar
  1/4 cup chopped fresh parsley
    1 lime, quartered, for serving (optional)

1. In a medium saucepan, heat 2 tablespoons of the oil over moderately low heat. Add the onion and cook, stirring occasionally, until translucent, about 5 minutes. Stir in the garlic, turmeric, cumin, 1 teaspoon of the salt, the black pepper, and rice. Cook, stirring frequently, for 2 minutes.

2. Add the water and bay leaf; bring to a simmer. Reduce the heat to low and cook, covered, until all the liquid is absorbed and the rice is done, about 20 minutes. Remove the bay leaf.

3. In a large glass or stainless-steel bowl, combine the rice, beans, bell pepper, and tomatoes. Add the remaining 1 tablespoon oil and 1/4 teaspoon salt, the vinegar, and parsley. Toss gently to combine. Serve with lime wedges, if using.

VEGETABLE TIP

Green **bell peppers** that are allowed to ripen further become red bell peppers. This extra ripeness from additional time on the vine is why red peppers are sweeter than green ones, and also why they're more expensive.

GRILLED MUSHROOM KABOBS AND COUSCOUS SALAD

Meaty mushrooms marinated in a flavorful soy-sauce mixture, grilled or broiled to perfection, and served over lemony couscous salad make an altogether elegant dish. Kabobs and salad are also perfect picnic fare. Put the salad together ahead of time and throw the mushrooms on the grill shortly before serving.

WINE RECOMMENDATION
We don't often think of sparkling wine as an accompaniment to food; its usual place is as an aperitif. Here, however, a rosé Champagne, with its crisp acidity, hint of red fruit, and subtle earthy undertow, will be truly exciting.

SERVES 4

6   tablespoons cooking oil
½   teaspoon ground coriander
1   tablespoon soy sauce
1   clove garlic, minced
2½ teaspoons salt
½   teaspoon fresh-ground black pepper
6   large mushrooms (about 1 pound in all), halved
2⅔ cups water
2⅔ cups couscous
4   scallions including green tops, sliced
1   cucumber, peeled, halved lengthwise, seeded, and diced
12 cherry tomatoes, quartered
½   cup chopped cilantro
    Grated zest of 1 lemon
1   tablespoon lemon juice
6   tablespoons olive oil

1. Heat the broiler or grill. In a medium bowl, combine the cooking oil, coriander, soy sauce, garlic, ½ teaspoon salt, and the pepper. Mix well. Add the mushrooms; coat thoroughly.

2. In a medium saucepan, bring the water to a boil. Stir in the couscous. Cover, remove from the heat, and let stand 5 minutes. Fluff with a fork and transfer to a bowl.

3. Add the scallions, cucumber, tomatoes, cilantro, lemon zest, lemon juice, olive oil, and the remaining 2 teaspoons of salt to the couscous. Toss to combine.

4. Divide the mushrooms among four skewers. Broil or grill the mushrooms, turning occasionally, until they are tender and golden brown, about 10 minutes. Serve over the couscous.

Eggplant, Lentil, and Bulgur Salad

It's two salads in one—a hearty, spicy mixture of lentils and eggplant and a crisp, cool combination of cucumber and tomato. Each is fine by itself, but they're even better when served together.

WINE RECOMMENDATION
A rich, jammy red wine, thick with fruit and lush on the palate, is just what is called for here. Turn to Australia for a shiraz or cabernet-sauvignon and shiraz blend.

SERVES 4

- 1 cup lentils
- 5 cups water
- 2 teaspoons salt
- 1 cup bulgur
- 5 tablespoons olive oil
- 1 onion, chopped
- 1 eggplant, peeled, quartered, and sliced thin
- 3 tablespoons tomato paste
- ½ teaspoon Tabasco sauce
- 4 scallions, white bulbs only, sliced
- 1 cup chopped fresh parsley
- 1 cucumber, peeled, halved lengthwise, seeded, and diced
- 1 tomato, diced

1. In a medium saucepan, combine the lentils, 3½ cups of the water, and 1 teaspoon of the salt. Bring to a boil, reduce the heat, and simmer, partially covered, for 10 minutes. Stir in the bulgur and continue cooking, partially covered, stirring occasionally, until the lentils and bulgur are just done, about 15 minutes. Remove from the heat and let sit, partially covered, for 5 minutes.

2. Meanwhile, in a large nonstick frying pan, heat 3 tablespoons of the oil over moderate heat. Add the onion and cook, stirring occasionally, until translucent, about 5 minutes. Add the remaining 2 tablespoons of oil and the eggplant and cook, stirring, for 2 minutes. Stir in the tomato paste and the remaining 1½ cups of water and 1 teaspoon of salt. Bring to a simmer and cook, stirring occasionally, until the eggplant is very tender and no liquid remains in the pan, about 20 minutes.

3. Remove the pan from the heat and stir the lentil mixture, Tabasco, scallions, and half the parsley into the eggplant.

4. In a small bowl, combine the remaining parsley with the cucumber and tomato. Serve the lentils over the cucumber salad.

Sandwiches & Pizzas

PAN BAGNAT

The usual version of this Provençal sandwich is basically a *salade niçoise* on a roll. We've omitted the tuna and added fennel and chickpeas. Stuff the filling into hollowed-out rolls and let the delicious juices soak into the bread.

WINE RECOMMENDATION
Not only are rosé wines a perfect match for sandwiches, they're also delightful with foods highlighting the flavors of southern France. Try one from the region of Provence.

SERVES 4

- 1 fennel bulb, halved and cut crosswise into very thin slices
- 1 cup drained and rinsed canned chickpeas (from one 15-ounce can)
- ⅓ cup black olives, such as Niçoise or Kalamata, pitted and coarsely chopped
- 2 tablespoons drained capers, chopped
- ⅓ cup chopped fresh parsley
- 1 clove garlic, minced
- 1 large tomato, chopped
- 4 teaspoons wine vinegar
- 6 tablespoons olive oil
- 1 teaspoon salt
- ¼ teaspoon fresh-ground black pepper
- 4 large crusty rolls, split

1. In a large glass or stainless-steel bowl, combine the fennel, chickpeas, olives, capers, parsley, garlic, and tomato. Add the vinegar, oil, salt, and pepper and toss.

2. Remove some of the soft center from each half roll, leaving a ½-inch shell. Mound the filling onto the bottom of each roll. Drizzle any remaining juices over the filling. Cover with the top of each roll.

3. If you have time, wrap each roll tightly in aluminum foil and let sit for 15 minutes or up to 2 hours. Otherwise, press down on the rolls firmly so that the dressing moistens the bread.

VARIATIONS

Other delicious ingredients to add to the sandwich include strips of raw **green bell pepper** or roasted **red bell pepper**, sliced **hard-cooked egg**, a small can of drained **tuna**, a few chopped **anchovy fillets**, or a handful of fresh **basil leaves**.

VEGETABLE SANDWICH WITH DILL SAUCE

Stacked high with slices of tomato, onion, cucumber, avocado, and provolone cheese, this is a vegetable sandwich that even confirmed carnivores will love. You can add or substitute other fresh vegetables; radishes, spinach, or grated carrot go particularly well here. When you can't get good tomatoes, don't buy lousy, cottony ones; use twice the amount of lettuce instead.

WINE RECOMMENDATION
The grassy, herbal flavors of sauvignon blanc marry beautifully with dill. With this sandwich, the lighter and crisper the wine, the better the match will be. A Sancerre or Pouilly-Fumé from the Loire Valley in France will do nicely.

SERVES 4

½ cup plain yogurt

3 tablespoons chopped fresh dill

1½ teaspoons Dijon mustard

1 tablespoon cooking oil

1 teaspoon wine vinegar

   Salt

   Fresh-ground black pepper

8 thick slices multigrain bread

8 lettuce leaves

½ pound sliced provolone

2 tomatoes, sliced

1 cucumber, peeled and sliced thin

1 small red onion, sliced very thin

1 ripe avocado, preferably Hass, sliced

1 cup alfalfa sprouts

1. In a small bowl, stir together the yogurt, dill, mustard, oil, vinegar, ¼ teaspoon salt, and ⅛ teaspoon pepper.

2. Spread a tablespoon of the dill sauce on one side of each of four slices of bread. Top each slice with lettuce, provolone, tomatoes, a sprinkling of salt and pepper, the cucumber, onion, avocado, and sprouts. Drizzle another tablespoon of dill sauce over each sandwich. Cover with the remaining four slices of bread.

VEGETABLE TIP

If raw **onions** have too much of a bite, tame them by rinsing the slices under cold running water or soaking them in a bowl of cold water for a few minutes. Pat them dry before putting them on your sandwich.

GRILLED-VEGETABLE SANDWICH

There's plenty of room for experimentation here. We've used grilled eggplant, zucchini, bell peppers, and onion sandwiched in crusty rolls with a little pesto. Fennel, endive, or mushrooms would make fine vegetable substitutes; sun-dried-tomato or white-bean puree can replace the pesto; or omit the condiment altogether and top the sandwiches with whole fresh basil or mint leaves. You can even change the cooking equipment, using the broiler or a grill pan in lieu of an outdoor grill.

WINE RECOMMENDATION

Alsace pinot blancs are among the most versatile of wines. Soft, nutty, and easy to drink, they partner vegetables, chicken, and fish equally well. And most appropriately for this unpretentious sandwich, they are always inexpensive.

SERVES 4

1	teaspoon dried oregano
2	tablespoons chopped fresh basil (optional)
½	teaspoon salt
½	teaspoon fresh-ground black pepper
1½	teaspoons wine vinegar
¾	cup olive oil
1	eggplant, cut into ½-inch slices
1	zucchini, cut into ½-inch slices
2	red bell peppers, cut into wedges
1	red onion, cut into ½-inch slices
4	large crusty rolls, split
4	tablespoons store-bought or homemade pesto
4	leaves romaine lettuce
2	tomatoes, sliced

1. Light the grill. In a large bowl, combine the oregano, the basil, if using, the salt, black pepper, vinegar, and oil. Add the eggplant, zucchini, bell peppers, and onion and stir to coat. Grill the vegetables in batches, turning once, until lightly browned and tender, 10 to 15 minutes per batch.

2. Spread the inside of each roll with 1 tablespoon of the pesto. Sandwich the grilled vegetables, lettuce, and tomatoes in the rolls.

VEGETABLE TIP

Slice **zucchini** lengthwise for grilling, so that you won't have to contend with all those little rounds of squash threatening to fall through the grate.

BABA GHANOUJ ON PITA

The creamy Middle Eastern eggplant dip called baba ghanouj is traditionally served with warm pita and an assortment of salads. Here, we top the pita with the dip and a mixture of romaine, tomato, and cucumber for an extraordinarily tasty meal.

WINE RECOMMENDATION
Food-friendly shiraz is the daily wine of Australia, though many quite serious versions made for aging can be found as well. Steer clear of those blockbusters, however, to enjoy shiraz's lush blackberry fruit and supple texture with this recipe.

SERVES 4

2 large eggplants (about 2 pounds each), peeled and cut into 1-inch cubes

3 tablespoons olive oil

¾ teaspoon salt

½ teaspoon fresh-ground black pepper

8 pitas

¼ cup lemon juice (from about 1 lemon)

⅓ cup tahini

¾ teaspoon ground cumin

2 cloves garlic, peeled

1 small head romaine lettuce (about ¾ pound), cut crosswise into 1-inch strips (about 5 cups)

1 plum tomato, halved lengthwise and cut crosswise into thin strips

1 cucumber, peeled, halved lengthwise, seeded, and sliced thin

½ teaspoon wine vinegar

1. Heat the oven to 450°. Put the eggplant cubes on a large baking sheet and toss with 2 tablespoons of the oil and ¼ teaspoon each of the salt and pepper. Arrange the cubes in a single layer and roast, stirring occasionally, until soft and golden, about 15 minutes. Set aside to cool.

2. Reduce the heat to 350°. Wrap the pitas in aluminum foil, making two packets of four, and warm in the oven for 10 minutes.

3. Meanwhile, put the roasted eggplant, the lemon juice, tahini, cumin, garlic, and ¼ teaspoon of the salt in a blender or food processor puree until smooth.

4. In a medium glass or stainless-steel bowl, combine the lettuce, tomato, and cucumber. Add the vinegar and the remaining tablespoon of oil and ¼ teaspoon each of salt and pepper. Toss to combine. Spread some of the baba ghanouj on each pita and then top with the salad.

GRILLED CHEESE WITH SPINACH-AND-TOMATO SAUCE

Call it an adult version of the grilled-cheese sandwich—slices of country bread layered with mozzarella, goat cheese, and tomato-sauced spinach and toasted to a golden brown.

WINE RECOMMENDATION
Here's another opportunity to try an unusual wine: Saumur-Champigny, a vibrant, fruity red from the Loire Valley of France. Made from cabernet franc, it has a wonderful strawberry aroma and enough tannin to stand up to the cheese.

SERVES 4

- 4 tablespoons olive oil
- 1 small onion, chopped
- 2 cloves garlic, minced
- 1 cup canned crushed tomatoes in thick puree (from one 15-ounce can)
- ½ teaspoon salt
- ¼ teaspoon fresh-ground black pepper
- 1 pound spinach, stems removed, leaves washed well and shredded
- 8 thick slices from a large round loaf of country bread
- ½ pound mozzarella, sliced
- ¼ pound mild goat cheese, crumbled (about ¾ cup)

1. In a large saucepan, heat 2 tablespoons of the oil over moderately low heat. Add the onion and cook, stirring occasionally, until translucent, about 5 minutes. Stir in the garlic, tomatoes, salt, and pepper. Simmer for 5 minutes. Add the spinach and simmer until the spinach wilts and the sauce thickens, about 5 minutes longer. Cover to keep warm.

2. Top 4 slices of the bread with mozzarella. Spoon some of the spinach mixture over each, spreading the spinach to the edges of the bread. Sprinkle the goat cheese over the spinach and top with the remaining bread slices.

3. In a large nonstick frying pan, heat 1 tablespoon of the oil over moderate heat. Cook two of the sandwiches, turning once, until the cheese melts and the bread is golden, about 4 minutes in all. Repeat with the remaining 1 tablespoon of oil and the other two sandwiches, keeping the first batch of sandwiches warm on a baking sheet in a 200° oven.

SUBSTITUTING FROZEN SPINACH

If you like, use one ten-ounce package of defrosted **frozen chopped spinach** instead of the fresh. Drain it and squeeze out any remaining moisture. Simmer the spinach in the tomato sauce just to warm it through.

THREE-CHEESE PIZZA WITH CARAMELIZED ONIONS AND PIMIENTOS

Fontina, Roquefort, and Parmesan form the sassy cheese trio here. Their piquant flavor blends delectably with the pimientos and sweet golden onions.

WINE RECOMMENDATION
The cheeses and sweet onions call to mind sangiovese's crisp cherry and herb flavors and high acidity. For a change, opt for a lesser-known Sangiovese di Romagna instead of Chianti.

SERVES 4

½ cup drained sliced pimientos (two 4-ounce jars)

1 teaspoon wine vinegar

3 tablespoons olive oil

4 large onions (about 4 pounds in all), cut into thin slices

½ teaspoon salt

2 12-inch store-bought pizza shells, such as Boboli

6 ounces fontina, sliced thin

6 ounces Roquefort or other blue cheese, crumbled (about 1½ cups)

2 tablespoons grated Parmesan

1. Heat the oven to 425°. In a small glass or stainless-steel bowl, combine the pimientos with the vinegar and set aside.

2. In a large nonstick frying pan, heat the oil over moderate heat. Add the onions and salt and cook, stirring frequently, until golden, about 20 minutes. Remove from the heat and stir in the pimiento mixture.

3. Divide the onion mixture between the 2 pizza shells. Top each with half of the fontina, Roquefort, and Parmesan.

4. Bake the pizzas directly on the oven rack (for a crisper crust) or on two baking sheets until the cheese melts, about 15 minutes.

PIZZA CRUSTS

If you prefer to start with store-bought pizza dough or your own homemade dough, simply follow the instructions in Step 1 of the recipe for Mushroom, Zucchini, and Swiss-Cheese Pizza, page 171, to prebake the crust before topping it.

MUSHROOM, ZUCCHINI, AND SWISS-CHEESE PIZZA

The mushrooms and zucchini that top this tantalizing pizza can be grilled instead of sautéed, if you prefer. Whichever method you choose, make sure the vegetable mixture is quite dry before you spread it on the pie, or the crust will be soggy.

WINE RECOMMENDATION
Nebbiolo is the grape of great Italian wines such as Barolo and Barbaresco. You can enjoy its complex mushroom, spice, rose-petal, and strawberry flavors in a much less expensive Nebbiolo delle Langhe or Nebbiolo d'Alba.

SERVES 4

- 2 pounds store-bought or homemade pizza dough
- 3 tablespoons olive oil
- 1 zucchini, halved lengthwise and cut crosswise into thin slices
- 1 pound mushrooms, sliced thin
- 1 teaspoon salt
- ½ teaspoon fresh-ground black pepper
- 1 teaspoon dried thyme
- ½ cup dry white wine
- ½ pound Swiss cheese, grated (about 2 cups)
- ¼ cup grated Parmesan

1. Heat the oven to 425°. Oil two 12-inch pizza pans or large baking sheets. Press the dough into a 12-inch round, or 9-by-13-inch rectangle, on each prepared pan. Bake until the dough begins to brown, 10 to 15 minutes.

2. Meanwhile, in a large nonstick frying pan, heat 1 tablespoon of the oil over moderately high heat. Add the zucchini and cook, stirring occasionally, until almost tender, about 3 minutes. Transfer to a small bowl. Heat the remaining 2 tablespoons of oil in the same pan. Add the mushrooms, salt, pepper, and thyme and cook, stirring frequently, until the mushrooms are golden, about 5 minutes.

3. Return the zucchini to the pan, add the wine, and simmer, stirring occasionally, until the vegetables are tender and all the wine has evaporated, about 5 minutes more.

4. Spread the vegetable mixture on the partially baked pizza crusts. Sprinkle each with Swiss cheese and Parmesan and bake until the cheese melts, about 10 minutes.

EVEN EASIER

If you prefer to use **store-bought pizza shells**, such as Boboli, simply start this recipe with Step 2. Spread the topping directly onto the shells in Step 4, no prebaking required.

SPINACH AND PEPPER-JACK PIZZA

Though not everyone is wild about spinach, just about everybody eats pizza. So here, mixed with peppery cheese and a bit of smoky bacon, is spinach that the whole world can love. Defrosted frozen spinach is quickest, but if you prefer fresh, sauté it in some of the bacon fat before topping the pizza.

WINE RECOMMENDATION
This tomato-less pie needs a soft, fruity red with some tannin to balance the richness of the cheese. Choose a basic Australian shiraz for its plum and cassis flavors with hints of black pepper.

SERVES 4

  8   slices bacon, cut crosswise into ¼-inch strips

  2   10-ounce packages frozen chopped spinach, defrosted, drained, and squeezed dry

  ¾   pound pepper-jack cheese, grated (about 3 cups)

  ¼   teaspoon salt

  ¼   teaspoon fresh-ground black pepper

  2   12-inch store-bought pizza shells, such as Boboli

  2   tablespoons olive oil

  2   tablespoons grated Parmesan

1. Heat the oven to 425°. In a large non-stick frying pan, cook the bacon over moderate heat until crisp. Remove the bacon with a slotted spoon and drain on paper towels.

2. In a large bowl, combine the bacon, drained spinach, pepper jack, salt, and pepper and mix well. Brush the pizza shells with the oil. Divide the spinach mixture evenly between the two pizza shells and sprinkle the Parmesan over the top.

3. Bake the pizzas directly on the oven rack (for a crisper crust) or on two baking sheets until the cheese is melted, about 10 minutes.

SUBSTITUTING FRESH SPINACH

If you want to use **fresh spinach**, remove the stems and then wash the leaves well and shred them. Cook the spinach in one tablespoon of the bacon fat over moderately high heat until just wilted, about two minutes. Squeeze out the excess liquid and then combine with the other ingredients, as in Step 2. Since fresh spinach cooks down to such a small amount, you will need about three pounds to equal the amount of frozen spinach used here. If you don't mind having less spinach on your pizza, one pound per shell is fine.

POTATO, CELERY, AND GRUYÈRE PIE

Not quite a pizza, not really a gratin, this unconventional Franco-Italian mix is hard to categorize but easy to love. The combination of bread dough and potatoes may seem surprising, too; yet it's common in Europe.

WINE RECOMMENDATION
Pinotage is a grape unique to South Africa. It makes a soft, juicy, berry-flavored red wine with smoky accents akin to syrah. A pinotage will be lovely with the Gruyère in this dish.

SERVES 4

3 cups canned low-sodium chicken broth or homemade stock

1½ pounds baking potatoes (about 3), peeled and sliced thin

½ teaspoon dried thyme

½ teaspoon salt

½ teaspoon fresh-ground black pepper

3 ribs celery, sliced

½ cup heavy cream

1 pound store-bought or homemade pizza dough

6 ounces Gruyère cheese, grated (about 1½ cups)

1. Heat the oven to 400°. Put the broth, potatoes, thyme, salt, and pepper in a medium saucepan. Cover and bring to a boil. Uncover and simmer until the potatoes are just tender, about 5 minutes. Remove the potatoes with a slotted spoon and transfer to a bowl.

2. Add the celery and cream to the simmering broth and cook, stirring frequently, until the celery is very tender and the cream has thickened, about 10 minutes. Add the celery mixture to the potatoes and fold gently to combine.

3. Meanwhile, oil two 12-inch pizza pans or large baking sheets. Press the dough into a 9-by-13-inch rectangle on each prepared pan. Bake until the dough begins to brown, about 7 minutes. Spoon the potato mixture over the dough. Sprinkle the cheese over the top and bake until the cheese and crust are golden, about 15 minutes.

VARIATION

Try some thin-sliced **fennel** instead of some of the celery. You'll need a total of one-and-a-half cups of the sliced vegetables.

SWISS-CHARD AND SUN-DRIED-TOMATO CALZONE

Warm pillows of pizza dough stuffed with cheese and other savory ingredients, calzone are surprisingly easy to make. We've added sun-dried tomatoes and Swiss chard to the cheese for a calzone that's a meal in itself.

WINE RECOMMENDATION
The sangiovese grape of Tuscany has a wonderful affinity for sun-dried tomatoes and ricotta cheese. It forms the basis of Sangiovese di Toscana and also of Sangiovese di Romagna, either of which will be delicious here.

SERVES 4

- 2 tablespoons olive oil
- 1 pound Swiss chard, tough stems removed, leaves washed well and shredded
- ½ teaspoon salt
- ½ teaspoon fresh-ground black pepper
- 1 pound ricotta
- ½ pound mozzarella, grated (about 2 cups)
- 2 tablespoons grated Parmesan
- ¼ cup drained and chopped sun-dried tomatoes packed in oil
- ¼ cup chopped fresh basil (optional)
- 1 pound store-bought or homemade pizza dough

1. Heat the oven to 450°. In a large non-stick frying pan, heat 1 tablespoon of the oil over moderately high heat. Add the Swiss chard and ¼ teaspoon each of the salt and pepper and cook, stirring, until the chard is wilted and no liquid remains in the pan, about 3 minutes. Set aside to cool. Squeeze out any remaining liquid, if necessary.

2. In a large bowl, combine the ricotta, mozzarella, Parmesan, sun-dried tomatoes, basil, and the remaining ¼ teaspoon each of salt and pepper. Add the chard and mix well.

3. Oil a large baking sheet. Cut the pizza dough into four pieces. On a floured surface, roll or stretch each of the pieces into an 8-inch round. Spoon a quarter of the cheese mixture onto one half of each round, leaving a ¾-inch border. Brush the border with water and then fold the dough up over the filling. Seal the edges by folding the edge of the dough over and pinching it. Transfer the calzone to the prepared baking sheet. Brush with the remaining tablespoon of oil and bake until golden, 15 to 20 minutes.

Planning Your Quick Meals

Look to this section for practical help in deciding what ingredients to keep on hand, knowing when to find vegetables at their peak of flavor, and choosing what recipes to use them in. You'll also find an equivalents and substitutions chart and a recipe for vegetable stock.

THE QUICK PANTRY

If you keep staple ingredients on hand, you'll only have to make one short stop to pick up the fresh vegetables you need to complete the recipe.

CUPBOARD

- artichoke hearts
- bamboo shoots
- beans, canned: black, cannellini, chickpeas, kidney
- bread crumbs
- bulgur
- chicken broth, low-sodium
- coconut milk, unsweetened
- cornmeal
- couscous
- garlic
- grits, quick-cooking
- lentils
- mushrooms, dried
- oats, old-fashioned
- oil: cooking, olive
- onions
- pasta, dried
- pimientos
- pumpkin puree
- raisins
- rice: arborio, basmati, long grain
- soy sauce
- Tabasco sauce
- tomatoes: canned, paste, sun-dried
- tuna, oil-packed
- vinegar: balsamic, cider, red- or white-wine

LIQUOR CABINET

- cognac
- sherry
- wine: dry white

HERB & SPICE SHELF

- bay leaves
- caraway seeds
- cayenne
- chili powder
- cinnamon, ground
- cloves, ground
- coriander, ground
- cumin, ground
- curry powder
- fennel seeds
- mustard, dry
- nutmeg
- oregano
- paprika
- red-pepper flakes
- rosemary
- sage
- tarragon
- thyme
- turmeric

FREEZER

- bacon
- nuts: almonds, cashews, peanuts, pine nuts, walnuts
- pizza dough
- pizza shells, prepared
- tortillas: flour
- vegetables: artichoke hearts, corn, green beans, okra, green and black-eyed peas, spinach

REFRIGERATOR

- anchovy paste
- butter
- capers
- cheese: blue, cheddar, fontina, goat, Gruyère, Monterey jack, mozzarella, Parmesan
- cocktail onions, bottled
- cream
- curry paste, green
- eggs
- ginger, fresh
- horseradish, bottled
- jalapeño peppers
- lemons
- limes
- mayonnaise
- milk
- mustard: Dijon or grainy
- olives, black
- oranges
- oyster sauce
- parsley
- peanut butter
- pesto
- potatoes
- scallions
- sesame oil, Asian
- sour cream
- tahini
- yogurt

RECIPES PICTURED OPPOSITE: (*top*) pages 37, 83, 135; (*center*) pages 137, 91, 29; (*bottom*) pages 17, 67, 41

Vegetable Seasons and Sources

Legend: ▬ = Major Domestic Producers ▬ = Major Foreign Suppliers **Red Bold Type = Our favorite sources for high quality**

Jan.	Feb.	Mar.	Apr.	May	June	July	Aug.	Sept.	Oct.	Nov.	Dec.

VEGETABLE
RECIPE PAGE NUMBER

Asparagus 75, 91, 95, 145 — Calif., Mich., Wash. / Argentina, Chile, Ecuador, Mexico, Peru

Avocado 125, 135, 161 — California, Florida / Chile, Dominican Republic, Mexico

Beans, green 37, 113, 147 — Florida, Georgia, **N. Carolina, S. Carolina** / Mexico

Bok choy 17, 91, 111 — Arizona, California, Florida / Canada

Broccoli 19, 37, 55, 101, 147 — Arizona, California / *No significant quantity imported*

Broccoli rabe 93, 127 — California / Mexico

Brussels sprouts 21, 31, 145 — California / Mexico

Cabbage 31, 37, 79, 109, 113, 117, 129 — California, Florida, Texas / Canada, Holland, Mexico

Cabbage, napa (Chinese) 19, 111 — California, Florida, Michigan, New Jersey, New York, Texas / Canada

Carrots 21, 31, 73, 111, 123, 145, 147 — California, Texas / Canada

Cauliflower 37, 57, 149 — California / California, New York, Texas / Canada / Calif.

Celery 31, 117, 143, 175 — California, Florida, **Utah** / Canada

Collard greens 69 — Alabama, Florida, Georgia, **N. Carolina, S. Carolina**, Texas, Virginia / *No significant quantity imported*

Corn 25, 97, 113, 115 — Mexico / Florida / Mexico

Cucumber 45, 85, 147, 153, 161, 165 — Mexico / Florida, N. Carolina, S. Carolina / Mexico

Eggplant 35, 47, 49, 105, 155, 163, 165 — California, Georgia, N. Carolina, S. Carolina / Holland, Honduras, Mexico / California, New Jersey

Escarole 53, 117, 127 — Florida / *No significant quantity imported* / Florida

This chart reflects the availability of supermarket vegetables across the country. Seasons for local produce, of course, may vary. The vegetables listed here are grown in the ground, not hydroponically.

Vegetable	Domestic	Imported
Fennel 31, 113, 117, 145, 159, 175	California	Holland, Italy
Jerusalem artichokes 123	California	No significant quantity imported
Kale 23, 117, 119	Alabama, Florida, Georgia, New York, New Jersey, N. Carolina, S. Carolina, Texas, Virginia	No significant quantity imported
Mushrooms 49, 51, 67, 79, 81, 101, 139, 153, 171	Pennsylvania	No significant quantity imported
Onions 43, 113, 137, 143, 161, 163, 169	Michigan, Pennsylvania	Canada
Parsnips 31, 113	Calif., Mass., Mich., Wash.	Canada
Peas, snow 17, 37, 45	Florida, Texas	Guatemala, Peru
Peppers, bell 71, 83, 97, 115, 145, 151, 163	California, Florida, Washington	Mexico
Potatoes, baking 29, 31, 35, 121, 141, 145, 149, 175	Idaho, N. Dakota, Oregon, S. Dakota	Canada
Potatoes, boiling 37, 101, 115, 117, 139, 147	Florida, Montana, N. Dakota, S. Dakota, Wisconsin	No significant quantity imported
Radishes 17, 85, 125	Arizona, California, Florida	Mexico, Nicaragua
Spinach 17, 63, 77, 117, 127, 137, 167	California, Texas	Mexico
Squash, summer 71, 103, 113, 123, 163, 171	Florida	Mexico
Squash, winter 25, 27, 59	California, Florida	Mexico
Sweet potatoes 59, 119, 145	California, Louisiana, N. Carolina	No significant quantity imported
Swiss chard 29, 61, 117, 127, 129, 177	California, Florida, Texas	No significant quantity imported
Tomatoes 35, 41, 75, 83, 151, 153, 161, 163	California, Florida, Texas	Israel, Mexico
Turnips, white 21, 31, 109, 113	California, Colorado, Florida, Michigan, Oregon	Canada
Watercress 41, 135, 139	California, Florida, Pennsylvania, Tennessee	No significant quantity imported

Equivalents and Substitutions

The ingredient lists in our recipes seldom specify the size of a vegetable. You can assume we mean medium; for your convenience, we indicate average weights and volumes below. Because different manufacturers' package and can sizes vary, and even *change* occasionally (usually to hold less of the product), we've included the quantities you get from the sizes we used in developing the dishes in this book. And if you want to make a substitution—say you have tomato paste on hand but the recipe calls for puree, or you want to save time by using precleaned spinach from the salad bar instead of a sandy bunch of the greens—you can use this chart to substitute one form of a vegetable for another with confidence.

ARTICHOKE HEARTS	• 9-ounce package frozen = 2 cups • 14-ounce can = 1⅓ cups quartered
AVOCADO	• 1 avocado = 10 ounces
BEANS, DRIED	• 15-ounce can = 1⅔ cups drained = ½ cup dried, cooked • 19-ounce can = 2 cups drained = ⅔ cup cooked
BEANS, GREEN	• 9-ounce package frozen green beans = 2 cups = ¾ pound fresh beans
BELL PEPPERS	• 1 bell pepper = ½ pound = 1¼ cups chopped
CARROTS	• 1 carrot = 3 ounces = ½ cup chopped
CELERY	• 1 rib = 2 ounces = ½ cup chopped
CHICKPEAS	• 15-ounce can = 1¾ cups drained = ⅔ cup dried, cooked
CORN	• 10-ounce package frozen = 1¾ cups = kernels from 7 ears
CUCUMBER	• 1 cucumber = ¾ pound
EGGPLANT	• 1 eggplant = 1 pound
FENNEL	• 1½ pounds with stalks and fronds = 1 pound bulb only
GARLIC	• 1 clove = ¾ teaspoon chopped
GINGER , FRESH	• 1-inch piece = ½ ounce = 2 teaspoons minced
OKRA	• 10-ounce package frozen = 2 cups = ¾ pound fresh
ONIONS	• 1 onion = 6 ounces = 1½ cups chopped
PEAS, GREEN	• 10-ounce package frozen = 1¾ cups = 1½ pounds fresh
PEAS, BLACK-EYED	• 10-ounce package frozen = 2 cups • 15-ounce can = 1¾ cups
PUMPKIN	• 28-ounce can puree = 3½ cups
SPINACH	• 1-pound bunch = 10 ounces cleaned = 14 cups = ⅓ cup cooked and drained • 10-ounce package frozen, defrosted and drained = ½ cup • 10-ounce package fresh = 14 cups

TOMATOES	
	• 1 pound fresh = 2 large
	• 1 pound fresh = 2 cups chopped with juice = ¾ cup cooked to a sauce
	• 15-ounce can crushed in puree = 1⅔ cups
	• 28-ounce can crushed in puree = 3⅓ cups
	• 28-ounce can with juice = 3½ cups
	• 15-ounce can diced with juice = 1⅔ cups
	• 15-ounce can puree = 1⅔ cups
	• 15-ounce can sauce = 1⅔ cups
	• ¾ cup sauce = ¼ cup paste + ½ cup water
	• ¾ cup puree = 6 tablespoons paste + 6 tablespoons water
TOMATOES, CHERRY	• 1 pound = 3 cups
TOMATOES, PLUM	• 1 pound = 8 tomatoes
TURNIPS	• 1 turnip = 6 ounces
ZUCCHINI	• 1 zucchini = ½ pound

VEGETABLE STOCK

Our basic vegetable stock can replace the chicken broth in any of the recipes in this book. You can make it in a fraction of the time it takes for chicken or meat stock.

MAKES 2 QUARTS

- 1 tablespoon olive oil
- 2 large onions, chopped
- 3 carrots, chopped
- 3 ribs celery, chopped
- ½ pound mushrooms, sliced
- 4 cloves garlic, chopped
- 10 sprigs parsley
- 5 sprigs thyme, or ½ teaspoon dried thyme
- 2 bay leaves
- 2½ quarts water

1. In a large pot, heat the oil over moderately low heat. Add the onions, carrots, celery, mushrooms, and garlic and cook, stirring occasionally, until the vegetables start to soften, about 10 minutes. Add the parsley, thyme, bay leaves, and water. Bring to a boil. Reduce the heat and simmer the stock for 45 minutes.

2. Strain. Press the vegetables firmly to get all the liquid. If not using immediately, refrigerate for up to a week or freeze.

VARIATIONS

Good additions or substitutions include:

- celery root
- dried mushrooms
- fennel bulbs or tops
- leeks
- parsnips
- scallions
- tomato paste
- turnips

INDEX

Page numbers in **boldface** indicate photographs 🍇 indicates wine recommendations

189